GOOD NEWS

for the

BROKEN SELF

A SACRED INVITATION TO A HEALING JOURNEY

JOSEPH S. ARNOLD LPCC BCC

DISCLAIMER

This book is designed to provide information about the subject matter covered. It is sold with the understanding that the publisher and author are not engaged in rendering counseling or other professional services to its readers. If counseling or other expert assistance is required, the services of a competent professional should be sought.

Although every effort has been made to verify the accuracy of the information contained herein, the author and publisher assume no responsibility for any errors or omissions. The purpose of this book is to educate and inform. The author and publisher shall have neither liability nor responsibility to any person or entity with respect to any loss or damage caused or alleged to be caused directly or indirectly by the information contained in this book.

To Mom and Dad, Hazel Jo Smith Arnold and
Dr. Charles C. Arnold

You'll have to check this out of the library in heaven.
Thanks for everything. I love and miss you. I'm looking
forward to that great reunion in the future.

P.S. Take good care of Joe Jr. I greatly anticipate meeting
him for the first time when I arrive.

I'm not one who's got it all in place telling you what you should do, no, I'm just one old hungry beggar showing you where I found food.

—John Fischer, "Beggar,"
Dark Horse, Myrrh Records/Word Records, 1982.

'Ah, alas!' cried Glóin. 'When will the day come of our revenge? But still there are the Three. What of the Three Rings of the Elves? Very mighty Rings, it is said. Do not the Elf-lords keep them? Yet they too were made by the Dark Lord long ago. Are they idle? I see Elf-lords here. Will they not say?'

The Elves returned no answer. 'Did you not hear me, Glóin?' said Elrond. 'The Three were not made by Sauron, nor did he ever touch them. But of them it is not permitted to speak. So much only in this hour of doubt I may now say. They are not idle. But they were not made as weapons of war or conquest: that is not their power. Those who made them did not desire strength or domination or hoarded wealth, but understanding, making, and healing, to preserve all things unstained. These things the Elves of Middle-earth have in some measure gained, though with sorrow.

—J. R. R. Tolkien, *The Lord of the Rings*
(New York: Ballantine Books, 1954–1974).

TABLE OF CONTENTS

INTRODUCTION

"The Spirit of the Sovereign Lord is on me, because the Lord has anointed me to preach good news to the poor. He has sent me to bind up the brokenhearted, to proclaim freedom for the captives and release from darkness for the prisoners."[1]

Fast-forward several hundred years. Jesus was just beginning his public ministry.

> He went to Nazareth, where he had been brought up, and on the Sabbath day he went into the synagogue, as was his custom. And he stood up to read. The scroll of the prophet Isaiah was handed to Him. Unrolling it, he found the place where it is written, "The Spirit of the Lord is on me, because he has anointed me to preach good news to the poor. He has sent me to proclaim freedom for the prisoners and recovery of sight for the blind, to release the oppressed, to proclaim the year of the Lord's favor." Then he rolled up the scroll, gave it back to the attendant and sat down. The eyes everyone in the synagogue were fastened on him, and He began

by saying to them, "Today this Scripture is fulfilled in your hearing."[2]

Has something important been overlooked? If not, has it been relegated as somewhat trivial or relatively unimportant? Here are a few things to consider. Jesus was handed the scroll of the prophet Isaiah. He found the place where it is written, "The Spirit of the Lord is on me." Of all the passages he could have chosen, he specifically selected **this one**. But there is something missing from Luke's summary of the passage from Isaiah that Jesus stood up and read in the synagogue that day.

Let me give you a clue. Look right after the phrase, "He has sent me to..."

Many years ago, the prophet Isaiah uttered these words to describe someone who would come, whose impact would be truly transformative.

> The Spirit of the Sovereign Lord is on me, because the Lord has anointed me to preach good news to the poor. ***He has sent me to bind up the brokenhearted***, to proclaim freedom for the captives and release from darkness for the prisoners . . .[3]

What? Wow. Really?

My wife presented me with The Maxwell Leadership Bible as a gift a few years ago, which was in the New King James Version (NKJV) translation, a more readable KJV in modern English. I was reading in Luke 4 one day and read in verse 18 the phrase, *"He has sent me to bind up the brokenhearted."* I found myself somewhat shocked and surprised to read that phrase and thought, *I don't remember seeing that there before.* In my adult life, the two translations of the Bible I studied the most were the New American Standard Bible (NASB) and the New International Version (NIV). I consulted my NASB first. *The phrase was not there.* I then consulted my NIV with the same results. *The phrase was not there either.*[4]

There are several good explanations for why a portion of a verse may be left out when referring to another passage in the Bible.

Bible scholar Dr. Jerry Gladson was one of my professors at the Psychological Studies Institute (now Richmont Graduate University) in Atlanta, Georgia, in the early 1990s. Dr. Gladson shared some of his thoughts on these passages in a phone interview. He said, "It was quite customary in Jesus' day for a teacher to site excerpts from an Old Testament passage, while leaving out portions of it. This was the way of Jewish exegesis at the time. The citation in Luke simply illustrates that tendency."

While this was a customary practice, Dr. Gladson then added the following, "Jesus would have read the passage from Isaiah out of the original Hebrew in the synagogue that day. The phrase, 'He has sent me to bind up the brokenhearted,' was in the original passage that he quoted from and read."

So, while there is a perfectly good explanation for the omission, I believe it is quite unfortunate for many reading the New Testament in many modern translations today. Please note: In Dr. Gladson's footnote, the phrase "to bind up the brokenhearted" was included in the Septuagint, the standard Old Testament text in use by the early Christians.

Both prior to and after this phone interview, I pondered,

Could it be that a generation of Christ followers have possibly missed some of what I now believe was—and still is—a critically important part of the gospel message of Jesus?

Curiously and with all due respect, I do not remember being in a Bible study or attending a church service where the focus was, "How do we help facilitate Jesus's mission on earth to bind up the brokenhearted?" I also did not hear this message in the variety of churches that I attended in my twenties and thirties. Even growing up in a considerably rich faith heritage, I have at times wondered what it might have been like in the contemporary church if this phrase had not been omitted, especially in many of today's modern translations of Luke's narrative summary. For all the great good done by Christian churches around the world, is it possible that even greater good could have been done in this area? Would the healing of our broken hearts be considered a priority in the church's mission for all instead of just being viewed as a sideline for a few "unfortunate people"?

Jesus honored the Scriptures, but He placed them in context as He was addressing some of the religious leaders of his day. "You search the Scriptures, because you think that in them you have eternal life; and it is these that bear witness of Me; and you are unwilling to come to Me, that you may have life."[5]

It is my hope and prayer to not set off a firestorm of questions and criticism about a passage quoted in the Old Testament, which is included in some translations and omitted in some other, more modern works. As I was wrestling with this, the words of an old hymn came flooding back to me.

My hope is built on nothing less
Than Jesus' blood and righteousness;

I dare not trust the sweetest frame,

But wholly lean on Jesus' name.

On Christ, the solid Rock, I stand;

All other ground is sinking sand,

All other ground is sinking sand.[6]

The place in the scroll that Jesus read from that day in the synagogue is Isaiah 61 in our modern translations of the Bible. Jesus was crystal clear in Luke's narrative that he was the fulfillment of this passage that he stood up and read, "Today this scripture is fulfilled in your hearing."

Here is the full text of the portion of Isaiah 61 summarized previously in Luke 4.

The Spirit of the sovereign Lord is on me, because the Lord has anointed me to proclaim the good news to the poor. He has sent me to bind up the brokenhearted, to proclaim freedom for the captives and release from darkness for the prisoners[7], to proclaim the year of the Lord's favor...

So, what does it really mean when Jesus said, "He (God) has sent me to bind up the brokenhearted?" How does this happen, and what does it look like? Can broken hearts be mended like broken bones? Is the possibility of substantial healing of our brokenness even available in this lifetime?

For most of my personal journey and experience, I did not believe that significant healing of our broken hearts was possible in this life. Or it might be available to others but somehow not for me. Have you ever asked in a moment of disappointment or discouragement,

"What's wrong with me that I can't seem to be as happy or together as others appear around me?" What if instead of thinking some part of our personality or aspect of our faith is defective, we may really be broken instead?

So, What's the Big Deal?

Some of you may be thinking, *Come on, Joe. What's the big deal about getting our hearts broken? It happens to everyone at some point. You just have to get over it and move on.* In all honesty, do we really get over it and move on as well as many of us think or act like we have?

Psychologist Mark Baker tells the story of a client who came in and announced in his first session that he did not want to talk about any of his past, which he believed was 'dead and buried'.

To this client's surprise, Dr. Baker replied, "I agree with you completely. If something is dead and buried, then I see no reason for beating a dead horse." When this new client paused, not quite knowing how to respond, Dr. Baker continued, "But sometimes we bury things alive."[8]

Could this be true of you or I? Is it possible that painful experiences in our past that we thought were dead and buried are not really dead at all? I never cease to be amazed in my work as a professional counselor when a client brings up an old memory that it is often still quite upsetting and distressing. For some, the mental and emotional pain still connected to the memory is almost as intense as it was when it happened roughly twenty, thirty, or forty years ago.

I have seen this repeatedly, plus experienced firsthand that the old adage, "Time heals all wounds" simply isn't true for most people. What if this whole brokenhearted thing is a much bigger deal than we think?

The goal of this book is to hopefully stir your mind and heart to consider:

- This really is a big deal.
- There are many ways that we can experience brokenness.
- There is value to looking at and understanding your own story and how you might have been wounded along the way.
- Mental, emotional, spiritual, and perhaps physical wounds can still be adversely impacting us.
- There may be substantial healing available for our brokenness *in this lifetime*.

My own life experiences and what I have learned from them will serve as the primary framework of this book. We all have an opportunity to be the expert of our own story. I have invited many men and women—friends, family, colleagues, authors, counselors, teachers, professors, coaches, and life coaches to speak into my life and assist me in understanding myself and my own story. I owe a debt of gratitude to so many. I have also learned from every client I have had the privilege to serve over the past thirty years as a professional counselor. My sincere gratitude to them all.

Some of these experiences, circumstances, and events I will also share have impacted me both for good and for ill. The good that has come from some of the always imperfect—and at times broken—people who stepped up, shared from their unique selves, and allowed some of the goodness of God to flow from their life into mine has been a blessing so profound that words fail me to describe it. Like so many, my life also bears the scars of being wounded by people and life circumstances as well.

To address some of these wounds more fully, I began receiving counseling for myself as a graduate student at the Psychological Studies Institute in Atlanta in the early 1990's. I can still remember sharing with my counselor a therapeutic approach that I was considering using with a client to hopefully help them heal some past wounds.

He then posed this question to me: "Where you are thinking about taking this client, have you gone there yourself?"

Somewhat embarrassed, I had to confess I had not.

He then cautioned me with this response: "Be careful trying to take a client somewhere that you have not been yourself."

I have tried to screen much of the content of this book, as much as is humanly possible, through the crucible of experience. In the spirit of Ezra, I want to honor his approach. "For Ezra had set his heart to study the law of the LORD and to practice it, and to teach His statutes and ordinances in Israel" (Ezra 7:10, NASB).

While my personal experience is a primary source of information, I will also be depending on other sources as I write. While I may not have personally experienced many things, I have witnessed a great deal firsthand in my life, especially as a counselor. Another wellspring of information I have had the privilege of drinking deeply from is what I have learned from trusted family, friends, colleagues and many other learning opportunities from trusted sources. Much of what I have experienced and learned has been gleaned from both living and working in a rich sense of community.

Another source I will be using seems to fall in the area of discovery. As I explored some definitions of some ancient and more contemporary words and phrases, it was as if I had stumbled upon a treasure trove that seemed to hold profound depth and meaning. It is beyond the scope of this book to fully develop the extent of brokenness in every dimension that will be mentioned. Several potential healing approaches that I am familiar with will be presented, but this book will not be an exhaustive look at all forms of healing.

Other seekers of truth may have previously written about what has seemed like discovery to me. If that be the case, it is my heartfelt desire to offer what I hope is a distinctive perspective that reflects the uniquely formed vessel and voice that the Father is continually shaping me to become.

I am quite confident that most who read this will either personally benefit from my story or know someone in your circle of influence who can. I believe some of the themes I will be discussing are universal, hence, impacting us all. For instance, no one gets out of this life without being wounded in some way, shape, or form. We live in an imperfect world with imperfect people. Getting wounded is inevitable.

I am honored that you picked up this book. An angel named Clarence once said,

"Strange, isn't it? Each man's life touches so many other lives."[9]

For good, for ill, or sometimes for both. Could it be possible that you are struggling with brokenness in some area of your life? Even if you are skeptical or becoming mildly curious, let me encourage you to keep reading. It is my humble hope and prayer that your life and the lives of those you know, and love will be touched for the good.

CHAPTER 1

THE ABSOLUTE IMPERATIVE OF PERSONAL RESPONSIBILITY

I want to be clear from the outset that just because our hearts have been broken, this does not somehow entitle us to be bad actors or actresses and participate in destructive behavior to ourselves or others. We are always, and in every way, completely responsible for our behavior—or lack of it. When we are wounded, there seems to be a tremendous tendency fostered within us to want to blame or strike out against something or someone. While other people and circumstances of life may have hurt us severely, I have personally experienced and witnessed that blame just serves to keep us stuck in our pain. While seeking to understand our own wounds and those of others can create a context for the occurrence of misbehavior, it is never an excuse for acting badly or treating someone else poorly.

Again, while some *explanations* can be offered within the context of the behavior, *they are not excuses* for behavior that is destructive to self or others. Though people and circumstances may have wounded us deeply, it is our responsibility to care for our wounded selves and seek out the help we need.

> *"If we do not transform our pain, we will most assuredly transmit it."*

Richard Rohr

Psychologist and author Sandra Wilson aptly titled one of her books *Hurt People, Hurt People*. Undoubtedly, many of us have had a personal experience that has confirmed this is true. Jesus' penetrating question to the paralytic at the pool of Bethesda is applicable to all who have been wounded. He asked, "Do you want to be healed?"

Will we continue to use our wounded state to make excuses for how we do or do not act? Or will we have the courage to finally get help for ourselves and take the appropriate steps to receive the healing we need?[10]

It is my sincere hope and prayer that, as you read this book, you may be open to allowing your heart to be healed and restored in ways you may have never imagined before. One of the only things to lose is a lot of the pain you may be walking around with. Ponder again this profound question that Jesus asked:

Do you want to be healed?

CHAPTER 2

WHY YOU MAY HAVE A DIFFICULT TIME BENEFITING FROM THIS BOOK

The range of what we think and do is limited by what we fail to notice and because we fail to notice that we fail to notice there is little we can do to change until we notice how failing to notice shapes our thoughts and desires.

R. D. Laing

"He who has ears, let him hear." (Matthew 13:9 NIV).

"In them is fulfilled the prophecy of Isaiah: 'You will be ever hearing but never understanding; you will be ever seeing but never perceiving. For this people's heart has become calloused; they hardly hear with their ears, and they have closed their eyes. Otherwise they might see with their eyes, hear with their ears, **understand with their hearts and turn, and I would heal them.**' [emphasis added]" (Matthew 13:14–15 NIV)

Is it possible that we may be physically able to hear and yet still not really hear? Can we hear and not understand? Is it possible to hear and not really listen with our mind and heart? Even if you are blind and/or deaf, is it possible that you can see and hear with the eyes and ears of your heart? Or not?

While growing up, my Dad would sometimes come back to the room my brother and I shared and start asking me a series of questions:

> "Are you a good listener?"
>
> My initial response would be "Yes."
>
> And again, he'd ask, "Are you a good listener?"
>
> My response would again be "Yes." (At this point, I'm beginning to get a little frustrated.)
>
> And once more, he would ask, "Are you a good listener?"
>
> At this juncture, I'm thinking, *I really hope so!*

Why did my Dad keep pressing in asking the same question? This was his way of saying, "This is important. I need your undivided attention and focus. I really need you to listen intently and try to understand what I'm about to say."

attention
. . . the act or state of applying the mind to something.

- a condition of readiness for such attention involving especially a selective narrowing or focusing of consciousness and receptivity
- consideration with a view to action . . . [11]

We all walk through this life with our own unique pair of rose-colored glasses. You may take some pride in your perceived sense that you are "completely objective," a phrase I believe to be an oxymoron. There is not a totally and completely objective person on Planet Earth.

We all have biases. Complete neutrality is a myth. The only hope for all of us is to at least be somewhat aware of our own biases. Even at that point, we then need to have a willingness at minimum to briefly suspend our biases and preconceived ideas to truly be open to any new information. Jesus knew this.

I remember taking a Bible class as a student at Cumberland College (now University of the Cumberlands). This professor had his doctorate in biblical languages, and if he had lived during the time of Jesus, he would have been considered one of the religious leaders of the day.

One day in class, with tears in his eyes, he said, "What keeps me humble is that most of the religious leaders in the time of Jesus completely missed him."

They were the perceived experts on God of the day, and when God appeared in human flesh in Jesus, the majority completely missed him. The very serious matter at hand is that this unenviable condition could happen to anyone. It is quite possible to be extremely sincere about what you believe and yet be sincerely wrong.

> Not everyone who says to me, "Lord, Lord," will enter the kingdom of heaven, but only he who does the will of my Father who is in heaven. Many will say to me on that day, "Lord, Lord, did we not prophesy in your name, and in your name drive out demons and perform many

miracles?" Then I will tell them plainly, "I never knew you. Away from me, you evildoers!"

Matthew 7:21 (NIV)

If you consider yourself a Christ follower, this realization should keep you humble about what you know—or what you think you know—about God. If you are not an apprentice of Jesus, my hope and prayer is that this may also help you to be humble as well.

Terrance Gorski once said, "Human beings have an amazing capacity for self-deception."

Blind Spots

Psychologist and life coach Georgia Schaffer has identified the following four common mental blind spots[12]:

- We think we are the exception to the rule.
- We prefer fantasy instead of the pain of reality.
- We focus on a few details and miss the big picture.
- We do not know what it is we do not know.

No one is immune to blind spots. I think Mark Baker, PhD, licensed clinical psychologist and marriage and family therapist, said it well:

His (Jesus') harshest criticisms were leveled at religious teachers, yet he was one himself. You see, he did not criticize them for their knowledge, but rather for their arrogance. To him, knowledge becomes toxic when people cease to be teachable. The more we learn, the more we should realize how much there is that we don't yet know. Arrogance is a sign of insecurity and only proves a lack of self-knowledge on the part of those who display it. Jesus understood that human ideas are crude approximations of the universe—his psychologically brilliant teaching style always took this into account. I believe we need to learn what Jesus knew about the relationship between knowledge and humility if we want to be more effective communicators. Truly great thinkers are humble about what they know. They realize life isn't as much about knowledge as it is about faith.[13]

While a graduate student in my early thirties—I was a late bloomer—my wife and I attended Second Ponce de Leon Baptist Church in Atlanta. The senior pastor at that time was a gifted and caring minister and preacher. In a Sunday morning worship service, he commented that his adult son was getting his doctorate in philosophy.

He then said something to the effect, "I truly believe what God has to offer us through Christ is the hope of the world, but I told my son that if he finds a philosophy he believes has a better answer and if he can convince me, I'll join him!"

I thought to myself, *Did he just say that? Incredible.* I'm guessing this pastor had to be at least in his mid to late fifties. Was he still really that open to follow the truth wherever it led him? Would I grow older and remain that open as well?

How about you? Do you consider yourself to be teachable? Are you humble about what you know?

CHAPTER 3

THE CHALLENGE BEFORE US

In the middle 1970's, I was a part of a student movement that published a little booklet called, *The Four Spiritual Laws*.

Law One presents God's love and hope for us. Law Two presents the following:

*MAN IS **SINFUL** AND **SEPARATED** FROM GOD. THUS HE CANNOT KNOW AND EXPERIENCE GOD'S LOVE AND PLAN FOR HIS LIFE.[14]*

As a result of our sin, the booklet states ". . . fellowship with God was broken," plus men and women experience "spiritual separation from God."

Separation from our loving Creator. This sounds bad enough from an attachment theory standpoint. But what if the impact of The Fall, which has been a part of Judeo-Christian teaching for over two millennia, was and is far more pervasive that what is presented in this 1965 publication?

The organization called Cru published a very contemporary version of *The Four Spiritual Laws* called *Backstory*. (Here you can even find quotes from Bono and Gandalf!)

A much more devastating view of the impact of The Fall, a view held by Francis Schaeffer that has been more widely accepted among many in the Christian community, is presented in *Backstory*. What if it is more than simply "spiritual separation from God"?

Francis Schaeffer's much more expansive view of the impact of The Fall *also* includes the following:

- Psychological separation from ourselves resulting in an inner brokenness, which can result in the extremes of either inordinate self-love or self-hatred, plus other psychological challenges.
- Physical separation resulting in pain and sickness, plus the division of body and spirit, ultimately broken in death.
- Social separation from each other resulting in relational brokenness.
- Environmental separation resulting in stewardship violations and destruction.

It is extremely important to recognize that all these "separations" have a profound *relational* component:

- Spiritual separation in our *relationship* with God.
- Psychological separation in our *relationship* with ourselves
- Physical separation of internal working *relationships* between dimensions like body and spirit
- Social separation in our *relationships* with other people
- Environmental separation in our *relationship* with the natural world

This may be self-evident to many who are reading about these separations that lead to relational brokenness and the ensuing challenges that follow, but there is an inescapable interrelatedness in all these areas as well.

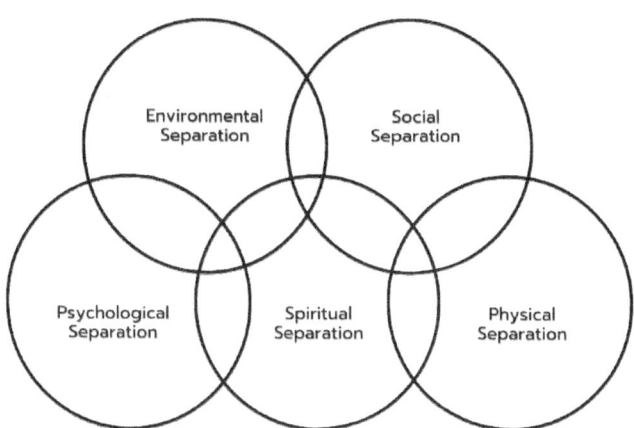

Current brain research has revealed that the quality of these relationships plays a crucial role in how we may experience healing, health and wholeness in all these areas. Neurotheologian, Jim Wilder, in his book, *Renovated,* shares an interaction he had with Dallas Willard about this novel way of looking at salvation:

> *Dallas's mind raced ahead of mine in our conversation about attachment. He wondered, "Is salvation itself a new and active attachment with God that forms and transforms our identities?" In the human brain, identity and character are formed by who we love. Attachments are more powerful and long lasting. Ideas can be changed more easily. Salvation through a new, loving attachment to God that changes our identities would be a very relational way to understand our salvation:*

We would be both saved and transformed through attachment love from, to, and with God.[15]

Most of the content of this book will be focused on approaches dealing with the healing of wounds in the spiritual, mental/ psychological, social and physical dimensions. The hope is that this will both engender and move us closer in our journey toward overall health and well-being.

Just take a moment and reflect on your inner world and the world around us. Could this view of The Fall help to explain a lot of the brokenness we see in the world in which we live? As you observe your own reality, do these "separations," many times resulting in various types of brokenness, have a ring of truth for you?

Jesus Christ, through his triumph on the cross, his resurrection, and his ascension has overcome, is overcoming, and someday will overcome completely all these separations and broken places.[16] Even as we continue to struggle in this life with various forms of brokenness and separations, the entire Creation of God still shines with glimpses of awe, beauty, wonder, magnificence, and glory . . . for those who have eyes to see.

GRACE ENCOUNTERS

I stepped away from working on this book one winter day to run an errand and then decided to stop by Kroger's and get some coffee at Starbucks. As I was going in, I passed a man who looked familiar. Then on a whim, I called out his nickname in high school. He stopped in his tracks and turned around, and this *was* an old friend from high school. What ensued was an enjoyable conversation and a brief visit down memory lane where we laughed and shared a few stories.

I'd probably not seen this old friend in over twenty years. Was this just a complete happenstance encounter? This seemingly random meeting was, for me, a grace gift. Unscripted and unplanned, it was a blessing. I walked away from this brief visit with a sense of joy and gratitude.

Sprinkled throughout this book, like rain, will be examples of these grace encounters that sometimes interrupt our lives and show up many times in surprising ways. In an extremely odd twist, even painful experiences can be transformed, at times, into very unlikely gifts. These can be places where God is able to heal, refresh, restore, and/or redeem parts of our brokenness, even when the events that cause wounds are experienced and perceived as a very unwelcome visitor.

CHAPTER

WHAT DOES "BROKENHEARTED" REALLY MEAN?

Merriam-Webster's Collegiate Dictionary (eleventh edition) defines the adjective *brokenhearted* as "overcome by grief and despair." While that may sound strong and gut-wrenching, the word *brokenhearted* for the ancient Hebrews meant "to shatter, smash, break; the heart."[17]

Does this sound mild to you? It sounds potentially crushing and devastating to me. A friend and colleague recently said, 'It sounds disintegrating.' What does it mean that our heart gets shattered?

In the Hebrew language, there are at least six different words for *heart*. The term *heart,* specifically used in Isaiah 61:1 in the word *brokenhearted,* means "one's inner self; inclination; disposition."[18]

Here are some other facets of this "heart," according to the ancients, from several sources:

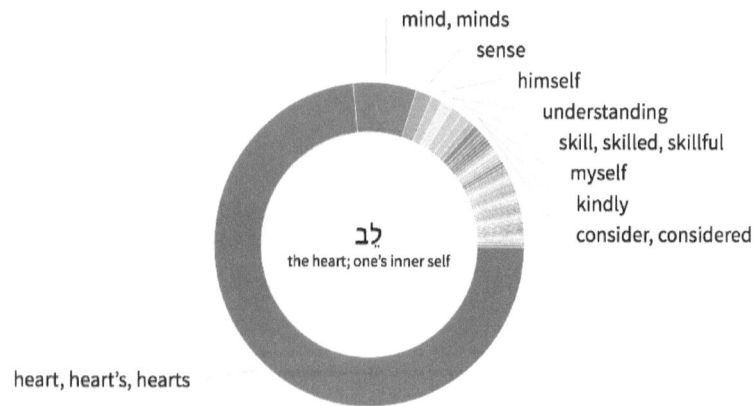

Lemma

לֵב lēḇ

noun, singular, absolute, common, masculine

- heart (internal feature): the locus of a person's thoughts (mind), volition, emotions, and knowledge of right from wrong (conscience) understood as the heart[19]
- the heart: one's inner self; inclination, disposition; determination, courage; will, intention; attention, consideration, reason[20]
- inner man, mind, will, heart[21]
- heart: mind, character, disposition, inclination, loyalty, concern, determination, courage, morale, intention, purpose, attention, consideration, understanding, conscience, interior, middle, life, person[22]

Did you catch all those different dimensions of the self that can get broken? What again gets shattered and smashed? *One's inner self.*

If a bone is shattered, it may take weeks or months to heal. How long would it take to heal a shattered self? It may seem so daunting at times that we may wonder if it's even possible. It may be easier to gain a more complete sense of what specifically can get broken if each area is listed separately.

- heart
- one's inner self
- inclination
- disposition
- determination
- courage
- will
- intention
- attention
- consideration
- reason
- locus of a person's thoughts (mind)
- volition
- emotions
- knowledge of right from wrong (conscience)
- character
- loyalty
- concern
- morale
- purpose
- understanding
- interior

- middle
- life
- person

When I first saw all these different aspects of the inner self that can be broken and damaged, it was mind-boggling. The potential extent and magnitude of brokenness was almost overwhelming.

While writing, I have felt many times that I am only scratching the surface of the breadth and depth of the possibilities of brokenness. But at the same time, my excitement about the potential for specific forms of healing—plus the hope and challenge of possible restoration—grew as well.

I have both experienced and witnessed—and am still experiencing—healing of brokenness in some of these areas in my own personal journey. I have witnessed healing of specific instances of brokenness in the lives of others I have had the privilege of serving over the years.

It is beyond the scope of this book to exhaustively explore how brokenness in each of the aforementioned areas may be specifically addressed. With that being said, here are some of the questions I've pondered along the way:

- Is it possible that many of these areas could be substantially mended simultaneously?
- If Jesus came to bind up the brokenhearted, what might an approach to healing in some of these aspects or dimensions of our broken selves look like?
- How might we be involved in this process as laborers with Christ in binding up the brokenhearted?

- Could it be that the failure to recognize and then seek healing specifically for our shattered selves is why so many followers and non-followers struggle so much?
- What if we have both a sin problem and a brokenness problem?

Are you beginning to get the picture that our true heart, which is really our inner self, extends far beyond just the physical pump within our chest or the emotional pain we may feel in relational distress? One's inner self, inclination, and disposition are powerful words that speak to the depths of our being, including who we are as people. If one's inner self can be shattered and broken, then the potential damage could be much more extensive and pervasive than many of us could have previously imagined.

Something to Ponder . . .

Christian theology teaches us that
We are all created in the image of God.
It also teaches that
We are all sinners as a result of The Fall.
What if also
We are all broken or can be broken,
To varying degrees,
Sometimes imperceptible.
Almost invariably causing some distortion of our
perception[23] of
Ourselves,
Others,
The world we live in,
Our concept and view of God?
Be careful believing that this distortion of our
perception in our fallen and wounded condition is a
completely accurate depiction of
The real you,
The real them,
The reality of the world in which we live,
The True God.
What if traces or glimpses of your true self are present
in some form in your fallen and possibly broken state?
What if there is the possibility of considerable healing
and restoration of your true self?
Your truest self will continue to emerge as you follow
The Good Shepherd's healing path and actively pursue
The Sacred Journey.[24]

CHAPTER 5

OUR INQUISITIVE QUESTIONING GOD

Why all the questions?

Jesus questioned the disciples, "Who do you say I am?"[25] The resurrected Jesus questioned Saul on the road to Damascus, "Saul, Saul, why are you persecuting Me?"[26]

I make no apology for my writing style that asks so many questions. I seem to be in good company. In Genesis 3:8–13 (NIV), God asked the following questions of Adam and Eve:

- Where are you?
- Who told you that you were naked?
- Have you eaten from the tree that I commanded you not to eat from?
- What is this you have done?

One morning, as I was reading this Genesis passage, I was so struck by God's invitation to have a relationship, *by connecting through*

both presence and words, with the first family. He clearly knew what had happened with Adam and Eve and the serpent. After all, He *is* God. So why was He asking them questions?

A part of my counseling training was improving the art of asking open-ended questions. A single word or phrase, like "yes" or "I'm fine, thank you," typically can't answer these inquiries. Open-ended questions force us to think, ponder, and grapple with matters of the heart.

In our age of efficiency, many of us wonder why God didn't just cut to the chase. Why didn't He just get down to business by sitting Adam and Eve down, pulling out the first whiteboard and markers, and giving them a lecture of how badly they blew it? Just command and conformity or get disciplined if you don't conform.

But He didn't. Why? I believe He wanted to engage their minds and care for their hearts through drawing them into a dialogue *in the context of the cultivation and expression of relational attachment love*.

The real meaning of "discipline" is "to teach." God's invitation to dialogue was the first teachable moment in human history. I wish I could say that Adam and Eve did not experience consequences for their actions, but we all know the pervasive Earth-shattering impact that flowed out of their choices.

Could it be true God desires to engage our hearts and minds in a process fostering more healthy relational attachment love? If this is true, would you be open to this possibility?

"Ponder anew, what the Almighty can do."[27]

So, where are you?

PONDERING THE INFLUENCE
OF TEMPERAMENT AND
THE IMPACT OF A PHYSICAL
INJURY OR CONDITION

CHAPTER 6

INTROVERSION IN AN EXTROVERTED CULTURE

Our lives are shaped as profoundly by personality as by gender or race. And the single most important aspect of personality—the "north and south of temperament," as one scientist puts it—is where we fall on the introvert–extrovert spectrum. Our place on this continuum influences our choice of friends and mates, and how we make conversation, resolve differences, and show love. It affects the careers we choose and whether or not we succeed at them. It governs how likely we are to exercise, commit adultery, function well without sleep, learn from our mistakes, place big bets in the stock market, delay gratification, be a good leader, and ask "what if." It's reflected in our brain pathways, neurotransmitters, and remote corners of our nervous systems. Today introversion and extroversion are two of the most exhaustively research subjects in personality psychology, arousing the curiosity of hundreds of scientists.

—Susan Cain, *Quiet.*

I was introduced to this idea more fully when I completed my first Myers–Briggs Type Indicator,[28] either in college or graduate school. My responses on the survey indicated that I was an INTJ. My results revealed that the first letter indicated that I preferred *introversion* (I) over *extroversion* (E). So, what are they, and what is the difference between the two?

Cain reports that the research indicates that anywhere from one third to one half of all Americans are introverts.[29] Presbyterian minister and author Adam McHugh helps to clarify some of the differences between introverts and extroverts.

> Introversion and extroversion do not describe categories of people but to separate forces within each person. Each person has a capacity for looking outward at the world of people, things, activities and events (extroversion, my add), as well as a capacity for searching inward in the world of thoughts, feelings, imagination and ideas (introversion, my add). All of our personalities move in these two directions. But while human personality is fluid and our personality types seem to ebb and flow depending on the context and circumstances most people tend toward one side of the continuum. Introversion or extroversion is a *preference*. Just like left—or right—handedness, and we will favor one over the other to varying degrees.[30]

Since it was clear to me that I had a natural bent toward introversion, I was more than willing to learn more about this preference and how it impacts my life and decisions. What I learned helped so much in understanding myself and others and increased my ability to extend grace to myself and others as well. Also, in some ways it freed me to take better care of myself.

Adam McHugh describes three main features of introversion:

Energy Source

Introverts are energized by solitude. For the introvert, "Long periods without quiet refueling leave introverts feeling physically exhausted and emotionally hollow."[31] I can so relate to this! Before really grasping this, I struggled for years thinking there was something wrong with me, like I was somehow defective as a person.

For example, while growing up, I really loved going fishing. While I enjoyed fishing with friends, it was just as easy for me to grab my rod and reel and tackle box, dig up a few worms, and head off to a pond I could walk to by myself. Immersed in the sounds of nature around the pond, I felt drawn to the solitude. To say I enjoyed fishing alone from time to time was not a stretch.

In college, going to Florida for spring break with hundreds of other college students had very little appeal to me. I preferred going to visit my grandparents in Shelby County, catching crawdads, playing basketball, and going fishing with my cousins. Introverts typically prefer to spend time with a few close friends and/or family members, as opposed to extroverts who might throw a party and invite a hundred of their closest friends.

Even today when I go to a social gathering, after the first hour or two of interacting with others, I'm feeling somewhat drained. On the other hand, during the same time, my extroverted friends and family are building energy and feeling great.

Internal Processing

McHugh continues,

> Introverted and extroverted "filtration systems" are
> different. Extroverts have flexible and porous filters that
> allow much to pass without getting clogged. They can
> usually take in a much higher amount of stimuli before
> they become inundated.
>
> The introverted filter, on the other hand, is much finer and
> more rigid, only able to allow small amounts of stimuli to
> pass before it backs up. Introverts process internally, in
> the workings of our own minds. We integrate and think
> silently. Ideally, we like to be removed from external
> stimuli and people in order to process. Our thinking
> proceeds our speaking, which means we will often pause
> as we reflect and carefully choose our words.[32]

I saw an email recently where a leader was recommending his top
twenty books to be read by leaders this year. It seems obvious to
me that this leader is an extrovert. As an introvert with a much finer
filter, I read more slowly and tend to pause and reflect frequently.
I do good to read more in the range of two to five books per year
as a result.

Depth over Breadth

Introverts prefer depth over breadth. This tends to play out in fewer
friendships, a preference for "depth in a few interests,"[33] and how
we approach understanding ourselves.

> Whereas for extroverts, there may be no limit to the
> breath of their experiences and acquaintances they

can have, *for introverts there is no end in our journey of self-discovery* (italics mine). Introverts are experts in our internal worlds, aware of the strata of motivations, feelings and assumptions that determine our choices and behaviors.[34]

Driving on the interstate around Louisville, one of the local colleges had the following on a billboard: "Explore the world. Start within."[35]

Now you know that there is a high probability that an introvert came up with this advertising idea!

Common Characteristics of Introverts

- prefer to relax alone or with a few close friends
- consider only deep relationships as friends
- need rest after outside activities, even ones we enjoy
- often listen but talk a lot about topics important to us
- appear calm and self-contained and like to observe
- tend to think before we speak or act
- may prefer a quiet atmosphere
- experience our minds going blank in groups or under pressure
- don't like feeling rushed
- have great powers of concentration
- dislike small talk
- are territorial (desire private space and time)
- may treat their homes as their sanctuaries
- prefer to work on own rather than with a group

- may prefer written communication
- do not share private thoughts with many people[36]

Healing for Introverts?

Have introverts really been wounded through being misunderstood and compared to extroverts? I believe on some level this was the case for me. Psychologist Marti Olson Laney stated,

> Growing up constantly being compared to extroverts can be very damaging. Most introverted children grow up receiving the message overtly and covertly that something is wrong with them. They feel blamed—why can't they answer the question faster? And defamed— maybe they aren't that smart. 49 of the 50 introverts I interviewed felt they had been reproached and maligned for being the way they were.[37]

McHugh has given this considerable thought and introduces a healing path for introverts.

> Our healing prescription begins not in exploring the nature of our introversion, as important as that is; our healing comes in probing the depths of God's nature and discovering the identity and purpose he gives us. Our heavenly father knows us even more intimately than we know ourselves. He sees us with perfect clarity and is able to speak to those parts of ourselves that no one else can reach. Our hope is in his work of freeing us from the *false ways* [emphasis added] we identify ourselves and conforming us to the nature of his Son. We cannot find freedom in our introversion until we

embrace our primary identities as sons and daughters of God [emphasis added].[38]

McHugh continues,

> For genuine inward healing to occur, this understanding of personal identity must move beyond the intellectual level that comes so easily to introverts and descend into the realm of the heart. It's the divide between the mind and the heart that leaves so many of us *fragmented* and incomplete [emphasis added]. [39]

Those false ways can lead us to distorted views of ourselves, and fragmentation just confirms our brokenness and need for healing. I appreciate McHugh's prioritizing "probing the depths of God's nature" as the place to start for healing and restoration.

You probably have a pretty good idea after reading this whether you are wired more to prefer introversion or extroversion. If curious, you can go online to www.myersbriggs.org and take the survey for yourself.

CHAPTER

NORMALIZING SENSITIVITY

I f you feel or experience something more deeply, chances are you will be impacted by it more profoundly as well. Elaine N. Aron, PhD, related, "The old unspoken (and sometimes not unspoken) question, 'What's the matter with you,' can finally be answered in a way that makes sense and stops hurting. You are highly sensitive. The secret trait that you have thought of as a flaw all of your life is a flaw no longer."

Growing up in Owenton, Kentucky, some of my friends and I occasionally got into a little bit of mischief. On one of those evenings, we were running through the backyards of several houses, and while a good friend of mine was laughing, I was feeling guilty. Why was I feeling this way while my friend was totally cracking up? (I will not mention the names of the friends who were with me to protect the guilty; nor will I identify the type of mischief we got into because I don't want to give anyone reading this any ideas!)

Going to church services as a child and adolescent, I would be stirred at times, moved to the point of tears. I do believe many times it was conviction of the Holy Spirit, albeit magnified due to my heightened sensitivity.

As a freshman at Owen County High School, I was sitting in my first high school assembly in the gymnasium the last day before the Thanksgiving holidays. The high school choir filed into their places on the risers set up for them. They sang two songs acapella, "God of Our Fathers" and "We Gather Together." Something within me was touched deeply. I will never forget this experience.

A little later in life, I was sitting in a college classroom taking a two-hour accounting final and discovered after the first forty minutes or so, I had answered all I knew to do. I handed in my exam and said to myself as I was walking out, "Well, I've just failed my first class."

I still remember calling my parents later that evening and tearfully telling them over the phone, "I don't really know how to say this, but I just failed my first class." I guess somewhere I had an unfounded fear that they may no longer accept me as their son since I had failed this test. I thought, *I'm a failure*.

They both reassured me that I had not lost my status as their son. When I received my final grade in accounting that semester, I had never been so happy in my life to receive a D. Not surprisingly, I did not become an accounting major.

In my mid-twenties, I attended Williamsburg Christian Assembly in Williamsburg, Kentucky. We were worshipping in song. Tears were streaming down my face. It was near the end of the service. I headed to the door and left quickly because I did not want anyone to see me crying. I felt deeply stirred and embarrassed at the same time.

As long as I can remember, I have always felt and experienced things very deeply. It could be said I have a very sensitive conscience. Remember those rose-colored glasses I mentioned earlier that we all have? My lenses are not only rose colored but highly sensitive as well. I have experienced my entire life with a rather sensitive pair of rose-colored glasses. (Note: Please keep this in mind as you read the rest of this book.)

If you ever had a class in basic or developmental psychology, you very well could come across the New York Longitudinal Study by psychiatrists Chess and Thomas. The researchers identified nine different temperament categories, and each category was on a continuum of low-to-high in each of these areas of normal child behavior.

Temperament is the expression of *how* someone behaves, "as contrasted with why the individual does what she does (motivation), and to how well she does it (abilities)."[40]

Their category that measured different levels of sensitivity was called Threshold of Responsiveness. Different children in this area could either be low, medium, or high in response to different types of stimuli in their environment. These would all be primarily experienced through the five senses.

We've all seen and experienced this as we've observed children when they get into trouble. Some children you can just give a firm or stern look, and they will burst into tears. Other children, this stern look will have little to no impact, and they will typically need something much stronger to get their attention (time-out or some other form of discipline).

A client introduced me to the work of Elaine Aron during a counseling session. This client reported a member of their family was an HSP.

I asked, "What's that?"

The client responded, "A Highly Sensitive Person. It has been researched and there is a book written about it." I am so grateful for the wealth of what I have learned from clients over the years.

The last week of January of 2016, I took the "Are You a Highly Sensitive Person" test/survey online.[41] I scored just enough out of the possible twenty-seven questions to be at the low end of the continuum to be considered an HSP. I know some individuals who answered affirmatively all twenty-seven questions on this survey, so on this continuum, some HSPs are more sensitive than others are.

Elaine Aron, PhD, author of *The Highly Sensitive Person*, comments on the research of Jerome Kagan, Harvard psychologist, who has invested a substantial portion of his life researching temperament traits.

> For him it is as observable a difference as hair or eye color. Of course, he calls it other names - inhibition, shyness, or timidity in children—and I cannot agree with his terms. But I understand that from the outside, and especially the laboratory setting, the children he studied do seem mainly inhibited, shy, or timid. Just remember as I discuss Kagan that **sensitivity is the real trait** and that a child standing still and observing others may be quite uninhibited inside in his or her processing of all the nuances of what is being seen [emphasis added].[42]

Aron's research estimates that 15 to 20 percent of humanity has this more highly sensitive temperament trait, another 22 percent were moderately sensitive, and 42 percent said they were not sensitive at all.[43] Please note that whether you are highly sensitive, moderately sensitive, or not sensitive, these are *normal temperament traits on a sensitivity continuum*. Aron states, "Having a sensitive nervous system is normal, a basically neutral trait. You probably inherited it." Neither is superior nor inferior to the other, just different.

Here are some common characteristics of those who are wired to be more sensitive:

- tend to be highly conscientious
- heightened awareness of subtleties and nuances in their environment
- able to concentrate deeply, best with few or no distractions
- better at seeing errors and avoiding making errors
- more sensitive to things in the air
- deeply affected by other people's moods and emotions
- often thinking about our own thinking[44]

The reason this is so important is that if you are on the continuum of an HSP, *this impacts how you perceive almost everything in your life*. The converse is also true. If you are not an HSP, this impacts almost everything you perceive (or not) in your life as well.

Knowledge applied is power. Whether you are an HSP or not, you can adjust and adapt your life accordingly, and you are the person primarily responsible for doing this. If you have HSP children, as a parent you are responsible for educating them and helping them manage this heightened sensitivity to their environment.

Please do not make the mistake of equating higher sensitivity with weakness. As a guy who is wired highly sensitive, I'm quite capable of being firm, tough, and even fierce in a protective way (not a destructive way) for those I care for and certain causes I may believe in.

I played American tackle football from fourth grade through my freshman year of college. I was never shy about going full out when blocking and tackling. In high school, our statistician told me after a football game that I had seventeen unassisted tackles. So even though I tend to be wired more sensitive, I was not overly concerned about how hard I blocked or tackled an opponent ... by the rules and legally, of course!

Want more? Check out this resource:

Elaine N. Aron, *The Highly Sensitive Person*, www.hsperson.com

PURSUIT OF EXCELLENCE VS. UNHEALTHY PERFECTIONISM

In my seventh-grade English/literature class, the teacher stated, "Today in class we're doing a timed reading." She explained how this was going to work (I must not have been paying very close attention). And then she said, "Begin!" and started the stopwatch. We all began reading quietly at our desks.

After a while, I noticed that the students around me were finished with the reading and started to talk quietly among themselves. This was beginning to cause some anxiety in me because I was one of the few who were still reading.

I leaned over and asked one of my classmates, "What page are you on?" When they responded, I quickly realized I was reading the wrong story in the book. I began to cry, and it felt like I had committed an unpardonable sin or the world was coming to an end.

Why was this experience so upsetting to me? Psychiatrist Richard Winter, MD, who identifies himself as a "recovering perfectionist," stated, "One key aspect of perfectionism is a sensitivity to making mistakes."[45]

Can the pursuit of excellence (a good thing) ever become unhealthy? Is there such a thing as a healthy perfectionist and an unhealthy perfectionist? I'll begin with Dr. Winter's description of a "healthy perfectionist."

The Pursuit of Excellence
adaptive, positive, healthy, constructive

- high standards
- good self-esteem
- strive for excellence
- realistic about failures
- organized
- energy and enthusiasm[46]

I rarely had to be pushed growing up (with the exception of a few household chores that my parents would ask me to do!) I wanted to excel in most areas of my life, especially physically, mentally, and spiritually. I came to learn that this trait ran in my family, to a greater extent on my Dad's side. Here are just a few examples:

- Dad was a perfectionist as dentist.
- My sister excelled academically and as a cheerleader. She earned an academic scholarship and became a dentist as well.
- My younger brother excelled as distance runner in high school, earned a scholarship in track and cross country, and has been a career Christian missionary in Thailand.

- Many other extended family members have excelled in their chosen professions and commitment to their families, through many loving, creative, and sometimes sacrificial acts. Plus, they lived out noble character qualities.

One specific extended family member, Lt. General Gerald W. Johnson, USAF (retired, now deceased) wrote the following in his autobiography,

> Next to figuring out what my instructor really wanted me to do in the airplane was to deal with my own inability to accept mediocrity. From my father came the desire to excel and willingness to put forth the necessary effort. I was the first one in my class at Chickasha to solo. I wanted to be the best. I studied hard in school and worked hard as a cadet. Still, I was always concerned that I wasn't doing well enough. The civilian instructors, experienced pilots under contract to the government, did not give us much encouragement. They were inclined to be very critical. If you did well, that was expected of you. If you did not do well, they let you know in no uncertain way. I found that flying was not difficult for me. Somehow almost from the beginning I seem to have a feel for the airplane.[47]

I always had a sense of this growing up. I wanted to do my best whether mowing the yard, playing sports, excelling academically in the classroom, or wherever. Working hard was clearly modeled by both of my parents. I've always been drawn to the words of St. Francis, "Do few things, and do them well."

Sometimes you may even get put down for trying to do your best. As a freshman in college in the Fall of 1976, I walked on the football team at the University of Kentucky. After the first few weeks of practice, I secured a spot as the tight end on the scout team offense. In practice one day, I ran a pass route full speed to the best of my ability, and one of the younger defensive backs attempting to cover me quipped, "Quit trying to be All-American!"

I thought to myself, *Yeah right! Quit trying so hard so that way I might not make you look bad in practice.* I just looked at him, not commenting, and ran back to the huddle. I had no intention of slowing down and performing less than my best.

Dr. Winter describes another form of the pursuit for perfection that becomes counterproductive:

Unhealthy Perfectionism
maladaptive, negative, unhealthy, destructive

- unrealistically high standards
- low self-esteem
- seek to excel at any cost
- generalize failure
- controlling
- exhausted and exhausting[48]

I've struggled off and on with a form of unhealthy perfectionism for a considerable part of my adult life. Making big decisions would literally paralyze me at times. The question, "What is the best decision in this situation?" would typically generate considerable anxiety.

I once attended a two-day professional conference on temperament where we were trained to use the Carey Temperament Scales,[49] normal for children and adolescents. I was just beginning to work in a private practice setting part time. I was hoping to use this newfound knowledge and research-based tools to help promote and build my practice. I had some brochures printed up to market offering temperament assessments. I became so anxious that "I might now know enough" that I never formally advertised this service. I think the brochures are still sitting in a box in our basement somewhere.

It was only a few years ago that I discovered through taking the Amen Brain System Checklist (now called the Brain Health Assessment)[50] that a region of my brain, specifically the anterior cingulate gyrus (ACG), was probably overly active. A targeted nutritional intervention with 5-HTP has been quite beneficial for me in this area. I now firmly believe that this deficit (for me, I believe my body was not producing enough serotonin) can be a considerable factor for some, possibly many, in the development of certain unhealthy perfectionistic tendencies.[51]

One example of an internal dialogue that I would have with myself would include, "I need to study more, pray more, prepare more, research more, think more, do more, etc., etc., etc." As an unhealthy perfectionist, it never felt like anything I was doing was ever quite enough. I think, on some level, I believed deep down that I always had to perform at a high level to gain the approval of others. If I failed to do this, others might not like me or accept me.

When I would hear about the depth of God's love for me, I had a hard time truly accepting and believing this. I know the old hymn says, "Just As I Am," but what if you feel that "just as you are" is never quite good enough? This opens the door to one of the magnificent wonders of the gospel . . .

> *For you are saved by **grace** through faith. **It is a gift of God,** not of works, so no one can boast.*

> Ephesians 2:9

Oh, to more fully grasp the wonderful grace of God for this struggle! I sang and read about it for years before its reality began to penetrate my heart more fully and completely. Some have defined grace as "God's unmerited favor." From my experience and the testimony of thousands of others, for this grace to be real, it must be tasted and experienced, not just understood as a concept or idea in your mind.

Want more? Check out these resources:

Richard Winter, *Perfecting Ourselves to Death*

David Seamands, *Healing Grace*

Brene Brown, *The Gifts of Imperfection*

GRACE ENCOUNTER: GIFT AND RESPONSIBILITY

"Come to me, all you who are weary and burdened, and I will give you rest. Take my yoke upon you and learn from me, for I am gentle and humble in heart, and you will find rest for your souls. For my yoke is easy and my burden is light"

(Matthew 11:28–30 NIV).

I learned what was for me a refreshing way of looking at these verses in a Bible class at Cumberland College. I am not sure which one of the Bible professors I sat under that was the instructor this day.

Come to me, all you who are weary and burdened ...

It is my responsibility to come to Jesus.

and I will give you rest.

I receive from Him the gift of rest.

Take my yoke upon you and learn from me, for I am gentle and humble in heart

It is my responsibility to take his yoke (teaching) upon me and learn from Him.

and you will find rest for your souls.

I receive from Him the gift of rest in my soul.

For my yoke
Responsibility
is easy
Gift.
and my burden
Responsibility.
is light.
Gift.

It was my responsibility and choice to go to this class at Cumberland College (now, University of the Cumberlands), where I received this gracious gift of insight into these verses.

Life places certain demands and responsibilities on all of us. This is inevitable and inescapable, and at times, these demands may seem to be more than we can handle. Jesus breaks onto the scene and makes this amazing offer to all of humanity. "Come unto me ..."

> *Weeping may last through the night, but joy comes with the morning.*
>
> Psalm 30:5b NLT

God pursues me with his love (gift). I repent (some grace here as well) and open my heart and mind (responsibility). I receive the gift of salvation. Salvation is a grace gift. I cannot earn it by working for it. But once I have received the gift of salvation, I am now His "workmanship, created in Christ Jesus for good works," which He in some amazing way graciously prepared for me to live in to.[52]

It is my responsibility to get into bed at a reasonable hour and sleep for a certain number of hours. Then I receive the gift of feeling rested and refreshed. "We thank You for these gifts we are about to receive from Thy bounty."

I pray. I receive grace from God. I practice other spiritual disciplines. I receive grace from God. I submit to God. I welcome Him in. I receive the gift of His presence and a greater tangible gift on some days of the actual awareness of His presence.

This book has already reflected this sense of demands, responsibilities, and wounds. It will be more balanced with gifts. Wounding experiences will be alternating with grace encounters. Difficult events are blended in with times of blessing.

Like many of you, I've had my share of challenging experiences in this life. In some strange way, there is a tendency among humanity to focus almost exclusively on the bad, the wrong, what's not working, and so forth. Just watch the evening news.

So, hang on for the ride. The roller coaster goes up and down, and so do seasons of life as well. It is my hope and prayer that your journey will continually be enriched by what follows.

IMPACT OF PHYSICAL INJURY

In the spring of 2017, I voluntarily underwent SPECT scans of my brain. The psychiatrist who interpreted my scans stated, "You really took a lick to the back of your head at some point in your past. Do you remember this?"

It saddened me to report to the doctor that I had no memory of this; nor did any of my early caregivers ever tell me that this happened.

The doctor continued, "You have an old, mild traumatic brain injury that resulted from the impact of this blow to the back of your head."

I was practically speechless.

I attended first through third grades at Owenton Elementary School in Owenton. There was a very tall sliding board in the playground area. Whether I was pushed at the top or lost my balance one day, I do not remember, but I do recall falling from the top of the sliding board, landing on the ground (probably picking up a few cinders), and "seeing stars."

I mentioned earlier my years of playing American tackle football. Although I was never diagnosed with a concussion, nor knocked unconscious, during this time, I know I took some shots to the head that left me dazed, "seeing stars," and confused for a while.

I was diagnosed with a seizure disorder in seventh grade. After I underwent the SPECT scans in 2017, a little later I began to wonder if there could be any connection between the old mild TBI and the delayed onset of a seizure disorder. I came across an article that said although seizures typically occur within the first few days or weeks after a brain injury, "some may occur months or years after the injury."[53]

From that point until my mid-twenties, I was on a daily combination of prescribed drugs Dilantin and Phenobarbital. Could the long-term use of these medications have caused any adverse impact on my developing brain during that time?

Especially when I was younger, I hated having to take the medication, and sometimes I would purposely skip it. I desperately wanted to be considered a normal kid. I remember getting a gentle, but firm lecture a time or two from my neurologist about the importance of taking the medication.

Some seizure disorders seem to resolve themselves quite mysteriously over time; others persist. I had a good friend pray for me specifically in this area in my mid-twenties, and I did experience a considerable sense of peace that day. I expressed an interest to my neurologist that I would like to have to opportunity to consider titrating off the medication just to see if I could remain seizure free, but based on my electroencephalogram (EEG), he was not in favor of this.

I found out through a mutual friend about another neurologist they knew and trusted, and it seemed like a reasonable idea to seek a second opinion. I went to see this neurologist, who said at some point in our initial evaluation, "I treat the patient, not the EEG." It may be helpful to add at this point that I never had a seizure during my waking hours. For me, they only seemed to occur while I was sleeping. This doctor allowed me to try to titrate slowly off the medication over a period of months, and during this time and ever since, I have remained seizure free.

Do I believe God is able to heal us mentally, physically, and spiritually? Absolutely. Do I believe it is a mystery why some seem to get healed in this life and others do not? Yes. If someone consents to receive prayer or another spiritual intervention for a physical or mental health condition, I would not advise that they just stop taking their medication or discontinue receiving other treatment without consulting their doctor or specialist first to consider this course of action. Seeking a second professional opinion, as in my case, may be advisable as well.

As a wise former president of the United States once said, "Trust but verify."

GRACE ENCOUNTER: PROBLEM OR DIFFICULTY?

I received this gift from a professor in graduate school, Dr. Kenneth Matheny. One day in class, Dr. Matheny presented a more nuanced psychological and spiritual definition of both a *problem* and a *difficulty*. Dr. Matheny defined a *problem* and "something that has a solution in this lifetime." Our approach to a problem is to **solve it.** He went on to define a *difficulty* as "something that does not have a solution in this lifetime." The approach to a *difficulty* is to learn to **cope with it or manage it.** A very high percentage of the time, a broken arm is a *problem* that can be solved. On the other hand, a diagnosis of type 1 diabetes is a *difficulty* that needs to be managed effectively.

The challenge for all of us is to be able to effectively distinguish between a *problem* and a *difficulty*. Sometimes we may get confused and try to **cope** with a *problem* rather than resolving it. We may also try to **solve** a *difficulty* and end up feeling perpetually frustrated. There are some injuries and conditions that we may not be able to completely overcome or substantially heal from in this lifetime.

The wonderful promise for the Christ follower is that if the injury or condition becomes or is a *difficulty* that we must cope with, we are promised that His grace "will be sufficient for us" (II Corinthians 12:9-10, NIV).

Can problems, difficulties and our environment influence the expression of temperament? Yes. Can the experience of a mild TBI influence temperament? Probably so. In all reality, each of these dimensions could impact the other dimensions. So instead of four mutually exclusive factors, they all intersect at some points. Exactly how and where they intersect and to what extent is unclear. For me, exactly how much each aspect of introversion, sensitivity, striving for excellence, and injuries influences the other will remain somewhat of a mystery this side of heaven.

10
CHAPTER

PHYSICAL ATTRIBUTES PERCEIVED AS FAVORABLE

"Know that the Lord Himself is God; It is He who has made us, and not we ourselves"

(Psalm 100:3 NASB).

Where I grew up, if you were over six feet, you were considered tall. I grew to be six feet and two and a half inches. I was a head taller than most of my classmates in elementary school. We played a lot of tag during recess, and I was typically one of the last boys to get tagged, if at all. I had good speed, was elusive, and could run away from most of my peers.

When I was in seventh grade, Owen County started a Little League football program. It was designed for elementary school children only, but in its inaugural year, they allowed seventh graders to play. Our team, the Bengals, made it to the championship game of the season. At the end of regulation, the score was tied, and we went into sudden death overtime.

I don't remember who won the coin toss in overtime, but we wound up receiving the football. I was back deep to receive the kickoff. The ball bounced a few times before it got to me. I mishandled it at least twice, finally picked it up on the third attempt, avoided a couple of would-be tacklers, and made my way to the sidelines. It was a foot race to the end zone, and I won.

The Bengals were now the first Little League champions in Owen County football history, and I was selected the MVP of this championship team. Athletics became a very comfortable and enjoyable part of my identity. Remember that phrase, "part of my identity." There is a considerable tendency in all of us to make some gift, some enjoyable or comfortable aspect of ourselves, our entire identity. When this occurs, we are all only a short step away from *seeking our whole identity in the gift instead of the Giver of the gift.*

For several years, there were rumors floating around Owen County that certain members of the opposing team could have caught me if a teammate or a referee had not gotten in their way. *Not a chance.*

If you think with those last three words that I might be getting a little full of myself, this is as good a time as any to insert this word of warning. I have become much more keenly aware of this, and rightfully so, especially for a book with the title, *Good News for the Broken Self.*

> Self-knowledge that is pursued apart from knowing our identity in relationship to God easily leads to self-inflation. This is the puffed up, grandiose self Paul warns about (I Corinthians 8:1)—an arrogance to which we are vulnerable when knowledge is valued more than love. It can also lead to self-preoccupation. Unless we spend as much time looking at God as we spend looking at ourselves, our knowing of ourselves will simply draw us further and further into an abyss of self-fixation.[54]

11

PHYSICAL ATTRIBUTES PERCEIVED AS UNFAVORABLE

Reckless words pierce like a sword . . .

Proverbs 12:18a NIV

Everyone gets injured by these reckless words, but for sensitive individuals like me, I think the sword penetrates a little more deeply. Derogatory words were said about my personal appearance in the first and second grades that lodged in me like poisoned arrows in my young soul. I choose not to repeat these words and phrases intentionally to spare more harm.

I was left with a distinct impression, "Something is wrong with me," and due to these differences of appearance, I had the sense that I didn't fit in well. I became a young child who was overly self-conscious about his appearance.

Oh yes, I heard the same words on the playground that every young child hears when they are young. "Sticks and stones may break my bones, but words can never hurt me." No matter how many times I've said this out loud or to myself, it made no difference. The words still hurt. Most of us learned quickly that this common childhood rhyme was a big lie.

Later, I'll discuss how a deeper level of self-acceptance helped heal some of these early wounds, plus the healing role and power of encouraging words.

GRACE ENCOUNTER: FUN

As I was getting ready for work one morning, I looked out a window into our backyard. I saw two rabbits just playing. One would rush toward the other, who promptly jumped up in the air, and the rabbit running ran right under the one in the air. They must have enjoyed their frolicking because they continued to do the same thing from different directions, over and over again. It was hard for me not to laugh and enjoy watching them having what certainly appeared to be pure fun. They were not resting, foraging, or running from a possible predator. They were just simply having fun.

12
CHAPTER

RECONSIDERING DOUBT

mind—locus of a person's thoughts

- that which reasons
- the doer of intellectual work
- the element or complex of elements in an individual that feels, perceives, thinks, wills, and especially reasons
- the aspect of a biological organism that is not organic in nature (in man, *mind* is experienced as emotions, imagination, or will)
- the organized conscious and unconscious adaptive mental activity of an organism
- the normal or healthy condition of the mental faculties
- the bent or fixed direction of one's thoughts, inclinations, or desires
- that which one thinks regarding something[55]

If you are wired to think more often, you are more likely to question more often. If you question more often, you're more likely to struggle with doubt.

Our minds are truly amazing. A great deal has been written about the mind from a variety of disciplines. Discussing one potential aspect or struggle like doubt will only scratch the surface of the depth and breadth of the study of the inner workings of the mind. Doubt can be an agonizing experience. Nevertheless, I've discovered it is not a rare or somehow abnormal struggle.

It was a Sunday morning. I was in the sixth or seventh grade, starting a Sunday school (Bible study) class with other age mates. At the beginning of the class, after our teacher got us all to settle down, she posed the following question, "Do any of you ever have doubts about your faith?"

Up until this point, I thought I might have been one of the only boys on the planet who experienced doubt. No one spoke up in response to her question, and it was completely quiet for what seemed like an eternity.

Then our teacher said, "It's normal to have doubts about your faith from time to time."

I can still remember the incredible wave of relief came over me. Suddenly, I was no longer somehow defective or weird just because I had occasional doubts.

Let me underscore here the incredible value of growing up in a healthy faith community. I am grateful for the mature teacher who demonstrated a healthy concern for young minds and assumed the responsibility of this role. Also, if my parents had not taken us to church on a consistent basis, I would have missed this considerable grace gift for my occasional doubtful soul.

Under the heading, "A Second Look at Doubt," Timothy Keller writes,

Let's begin with believers. A faith without some doubts is like a human body without any antibodies in it. People who blithely go through life too busy or indifferent to ask hard questions about why they believe as they do will find themselves defenseless against either the experience of tragedy or the probing questions of a smart skeptic. A person's faith can collapse almost overnight if she has failed over the years to listen patiently to her own doubts, which should only be discarded after long reflection.

Believers should acknowledge and wrestle with doubts— not only their own but their friends' and neighbors.' It is no longer sufficient to hold beliefs just because you inherited them. Only if you struggle long and hard with objections to your faith will you be able to provide grounds for your beliefs to skeptics, including yourself, that are plausible rather than ridiculous or offensive. And, just as important for our current situation, such a process will lead you, even after you come to a position of strong faith, to respect and understand those who doubt.[56]

I have been a questioning soul for as long as I can remember. It seems in some ways, I never really grew out of that childhood questioning stage, "Why is the grass green?" or "Why is the sky blue?"

Some famous people in the Bible struggled with doubt. John the Baptist, whom Jesus said was the "greatest man born of woman,"[57] was tossed into prison for questioning some of King Herod's "lifestyle choices."[58] In a moment of struggle in prison, John asked one of his disciples to go to Jesus and ask the question, "Are you the Messiah we've been expecting, or should we keep looking for someone else?"[59] Languishing in prison, John the Baptist began to doubt.

I think I was a sophomore at UK, and I don't quite remember how I got into this conversation with someone on campus, but he posed the following question to me, "How do you know the Bible is true?"

I was dumbfounded. I did not know how to respond or what to say. The best answer I could come up with as I look back was, "Because someone told me it was." I knew this response was not going to be good enough for myself or the student who asked the question.

This question set me off on a search, and someone told me about the writings of Josh McDowell. I was able to obtain his small paperback, *More Than a Carpenter*, plus his two-volume publication, *Evidence That Demands a Verdict* and *More Evidence That Demands a Verdict*. I then learned that the Bible could be evaluated by the same standards as other historical documents for accuracy and reliability. I discovered that through the bibliographical test, internal evidence test, and the external evidence test that the Bible is as trustworthy and reliable as any other historical document.[60]

Josh McDowell stated, "After personally trying to shatter the historicity and validity of the Scriptures, I have been forced to conclude that they are historically trustworthy. If one discards the Bible as unreliable historically, then he or she must discard all the literature of antiquity. No other document has as much evidence to confirm its reliability."[61]

As I was researching for this book, I discovered the original publication date for *More Than a Carpenter* was 1977, when I was a sophomore at UK. Was it happenstance this was published, and I discovered it when I did to help me (and probably thousands of others) through a period of doubt and searching? I think not. In the transcendent experience of the Christ follower, I do not believe this is an uncommon event. "You will seek me and find me when you seek me with all your heart."[62]

I believe there are some Christ followers who have the gift of faith, and they may experience little to no doubt in their walk with God. To have few or no doubts is quite normal for them, which at times can frustrate doubting types like me!

There are other forms of doubt that can be completely paralyzing, far beyond what I would consider normal doubts experienced in healthy faith formation. This is obviously not a beneficial or helpful form of doubt. I would encourage anyone consistently experiencing this kind of doubt to seek a professional counselor, wise mentor, or mature spiritual advisor.

IN THE GRAND
SCHEME OF THINGS,
IS THIS REALLY THAT IMPORTANT?

13
CHAPTER

PONDERING THE POSSIBILITY
OF PRIORITY

I have selected two focal passages, Isaiah 61:1 and in some translations of Luke 4. The phrase, "binding up the brokenhearted" is listed *second* only to "He has anointed me to preach the gospel to the poor." I hope to illustrate in the following examples a possible pattern of priority.

In Ephesians 6:14 (NIV) we are instructed to "put on the armor of God". What does Paul tell us to put on first? "Stand firm then, with the belt of truth buckled around your waist." What's next, or *second*, "with the breastplate of righteousness in place?" What does the breastplate protect? The answer is our heart, our inner self.

In the above-referenced passage, the belt of truth, breastplate of righteousness, and "feet fitted with the readiness that comes from the gospel of peace" (v. 15) all proceed taking up the shield of faith in verse 16. What if unhealed aspects of our broken heart can interfere with healthy faith formation?

Notice again the order: belt of truth, breastplate of righteousness (protecting the heart, the inner self), feet fitted with the readiness that comes from the gospel of peace, the shield of faith, the helmet of salvation (protecting our thoughts), and the sword of the spirit, which is the Word of God. Is it possible that our ability and capacity to truly be able to comprehend and receive the Word of God could be adversely impacted by damage and distortion in the areas of our perception of truth, plus the condition of our heart, readiness, faith, and thoughts?

This order seems like Paul's encouragement to Timothy. "But the goal of our instruction is love from a pure heart and a good conscience and a sincere faith" (1 Timothy 1:5 NASB). What if there is greater difficulty having "a sincere faith" if the individual has a potentially damaged and distorted heart and/or conscience? What if this further impacts our capacity or ability to love as Paul instructs in this passage? "Above all else, guard your heart, for it is the wellspring of life" (Proverbs 4:23 NIV).

A few years ago, I attended a men's breakfast at a church where I was then serving as the director of counseling. Our speaker that morning was a soccer coach from a major university who made this statement, "If you are going to *do* more, you have to *be* more." If parts of your inner self remain broken, are you truly capable of being more? Are you free to become the truest version of yourself if you are still struggling in this wounded condition?

14

RECONSIDERING THE HEALING OF OUR BROKENNESS AS A PRIORITY

"The Spirit of the Sovereign Lord is on me, because the Lord has anointed me to preach good news to the poor. He has sent me to bind up the brokenhearted, to proclaim freedom for the captives and release from darkness for the prisoners"

(Isaiah 61:1 NIV).

"So He came to Nazareth, where He had been brought up. And as his custom was, He went into the synagogue on the Sabbath day, and stood up to read. And He was handed the book of the prophet Isaiah. And when He had opened the book, He found he place where it was written: The Spirit of the Lord is upon Me, because he has anointed Me to preach the gospel to the poor; he has sent me to heal the brokenhearted, to proclaim liberty to the captives, and recovery of sight to the blind ... And He began to say to them, "Today is this scripture fulfilled in your hearing" (Luke 4:16–18, 21 NKJV).

Does the order in which we find divinely inspired scripture matter? What if substantial healing of our brokenness were intended to happen early on? It only appears *second* to preaching the gospel to the poor. What if the primacy of healing our wounds somehow enables us to see clearly and more fully embrace the rest of the mission? Are we truly free to "proclaim freedom for the captives and release from darkness for the prisoners" if we are still limping along in our wounded state?

The writer of Hebrews encourages us to "lay aside every encumbrance and the sin which so easily entangles us and let us run with endurance the race set before us."[63] Notice carefully that we are to "lay aside every *encumbrance* and the *sin* which so easily entangles us." What if unhealed emotional wounds are an encumbrance and are interfering with our ability to "run with endurance the race set before us?"

Do not miss that we are encouraged to address both encumbrance and the **sin**, and they are **not** the same.

The Bible begins with an orderly account of the creation story in Genesis 1. Did this order of creation matter?

In the 1980s, as a student at Cumberland College, I attended a storefront church, Williamsburg Christian Assembly, in Williamsburg, KY. One Sunday morning, the pastor gave a rather humorous illustration where *the order mattered* in the creation story in one of his sermons. "The young, gifted pastor said the God **did not** haphazardly say 'Fish!', and with untold thousands of fish flopping around, say in a panic, 'Oops! Water!'"

In the apostle Paul's letters to the churches, his greeting always began with, "Grace to you and peace." Grace *always* proceeded peace in Paul's greetings. Why didn't he switch it around at least one time and say, "Peace to you and grace"? *Because the order mattered.* He knew the experience of God-ordained peace is completely contingent on receiving, accepting, and experiencing God's grace.

Dallas Willard presented a defense that the order *does* matter in his discussion of Jesus' sermon on the mount (Matthew 4:17–7:27).

> To understand what Jesus is teaching us to do in his Discourse, we must keep the order of the treatment in mind and recognize its importance. That is what we would naturally expect when we realize we are hearing from someone who has absolute mastery of the subject matter with which he is dealing and is absolute master of how to present it. The latter parts of the discourse presuppose the earlier parts and simply cannot be understood unless their dependence upon the earlier parts is clearly seen.

Willard adds, "If we don't keep the sequential order of kingdom life in mind, as Jesus certainly did, it will seem that each new topic in his Discourse is being taken up on its own, with no connection to what has already been dealt with. The Discourse will therefore make little or no sense as a guide to what to do."[64]

So, what if the healing of our brokenness really *is* a priority? Remember, it only comes second in sequential order to preaching the good news to the poor.

15
CHAPTER

AN EXAMPLE FROM CHRISTIAN TRADITION

Are there examples in other forms of Christian tradition from the past that support this whole idea of the healing of our brokenness?

There is an invaluable storehouse of theology and the experiences of followers of Christ captured in hymns written over the centuries. The rich benefit I received from singing them in my formative years in church services is incalculable. Their lyrics and melodies still flood my mind from time to time and touch me in deep places.

I was attending a funeral recently of a precious believer who, like the apostle Paul, "fought the good fight of faith" and touched many lives in a meaningful way for the kingdom of God. Like many, she selected the participants, content, and order of service of her own funeral. The hymn she selected to close the service was "Victory in Jesus." While joining in the singing of this old favorite, I became immersed in some fresh wonder over the hymn writer's experience.

I heard an old, old story

How a Savior came from glory

How he gave his life on Calvary
To save a wretch like me
I heard about his groaning,
Of his precious blood's
Atoning. Then I repented
Of my sin and won the victory.
(Refrain).
O Victory in Jesus, My Savior forever
He sought me, and bought me,
With His redeeming blood.
He loved me ere I knew Him,
And all my love is due Him.
He plunged me to victory,
Beneath the cleansing flood.

This was the "gospel in a nutshell" that I grew up with. It was powerful, completely biblical, and transformative. The hymn writer continues,

I heard about his healing,
Of his cleansing pow'r revealing.
How he made the lame to walk again
And caused the blind to see.
And then I cried "Dear Jesus,
Come and heal my broken spirit."
And somehow Jesus came
And brought to me the victory.[65]

This stanza has a qualitative different focus, healing. The hymn writer then describes two examples of physical healing (lameness and blindness) performed by Jesus. Then there's a noticeable shift. And then I cried, "Dear Jesus, Come and heal my *broken spirit* (italics mine)."

Do you see the specificity of this follower's heart cry to Jesus? Not "save me," "cleanse me," or "forgive me," but "come and heal my broken spirit."

Read the next two words, "And somehow (... mysteriously ... surprisingly ... unexpectedly?) Jesus came and brought to me the victory."

My experience singing this old hymn on this day filled me with amazement. I had probably sung that hymn dozens of times in my life, but I do not recall the writer's cry of "come and heal my broken spirit" ever leaping off the page quite like this before. I immediately received this as quite an affirmation of what I am attempting to write about.

Do we have a spirit that can get broken? Absolutely. "The Spirit himself testifies with our spirit that we are God's children" (Romans 8:16 NIV).

spirit

> . . . *the immaterial intelligent or sentient part of a person: the vital principle in man coming as a gift from God and providing one's personality with its inward structure, dynamic drive, and creative response to the demands it encounters in the process of becoming . . .*[66]

Dr. Caroline Leaf has worked in the cognitive neuroscience arena for three decades. In her book, *Switch on Your Brain*, under the heading of "You Can Control How Signals Affect Your Brain," she says the following about our spirit:

> How? The incoming information is still in a temporary state. It has not yet lodged itself into your memory, or become a part of your spirit, which defines who you are. You can choose to reject the presently activated thoughts and the incoming information, or you can let the information make its way into your mind, soul and your spirit, eventually subsiding in your nonconscious and becoming automatized, dominating who you are.

I'll now turn to Dallas Willard for some greater clarity on what can get broken.

> Now, when we set aside contemporary prejudices and carefully examine these two great sources (Judeo-Christian and the Greek, biblical and classical), I believe it will become clear that "heart," "spirit," and "will" (or their equivalents) are words that refer to one and the same thing, *the same fundamental component of the person* [emphasis added]. But they do under different aspects. "Will" refers to that components power to initiate, to create, to bring about that which did not exist before. "Spirit" refers to its fundamental nature as distinct and independent from physical reality. And "heart" refers to its position in the human being, as the center or core to which every other component of the self owes its proper functioning. But is the same dimension of the human being that has all of these features.[67]

Back to the old hymn writer. Here is a repentant believer who seems to realize on some level that he is broken internally. I've heard more than one parent say something like this when they were discussing disciplining their child, "My goal was to bend their will without breaking their spirit."

Could it be that this really is more of the good news of the gospel?

"He has sent me to bind up the brokenhearted . . ."

And what was the result of the hymn writer's prayer? "And somehow Jesus came and brought to me the victory."

The church has taught for years that there is victory in repentance and believing faith. What if there is also a healing dimension of victory that was both written about and experienced by this hymn writer?

TOWARD A BETTER UNDERSTANDING OF THE COMPLEXITIES OF THE SELF AND HOW IT MAY BE BROKEN AND DISTORTED

16

THE IMPACT OF TRAUMA

Reber-Penguin Dictionary of Psychology reads, "Trauma—from the Greek word for wound, a term used freely either for physical injury caused by some direct external force or for some psychological injury calls by some extreme emotional assault."

In a "Trauma, PTSD and Grief" workshop, Dr. Linda J. Schupp, stated, "Traumatic stress is preceded by a trauma, a severe physiological or psychological wounding that is considered shocking and memorable. The word traumatic includes exposure-related fear and helplessness."

Mark Lerner, PhD, American Academy of Experts in Traumatic Stress, said, "Traumatic stress refers to the emotional, cognitive, behavioral, and physiological experience of individuals who are exposed to, or who witness, events that overwhelm their coping and problem-solving abilities."

After completing my graduate studies at Psychological Studies Institute (PSI) and Georgia State University (GSU), one of the biggest learning curves I've experienced as a professional counselor is attempting to incorporate some of the research findings that revealed the profound impact of trauma and how it can be addressed and treated.

Judith Herman said, "Memories degrade over time, but traumatic memories do not degrade until they are processed."

I mentioned earlier that one of the maxims I heard quite frequently while growing up was, "Time heals all wounds." As many of you who are reading will attest, this is simply not true. Not only does time alone not heal all wounds, but some people also actually get worse instead of better. This is never truer than when someone experiences or witnesses something traumatic. It may feel like an open wound for some time until its is treated properly.

My counseling experience has borne this out time after time. I received very little training in graduate school in both assessing and treating trauma. I now always ask the question, "Have you ever witnessed or experienced anything that you believe was traumatic?" I never cease to be amazed at how many people say yes to this question, and a considerable number not only report a single traumatic event, but multiple. For multiple traumas or persistent traumatic exposure, a new term has arisen in the psychological community, *complex trauma*.

When someone goes to the emergency room in extreme physical pain, an ER health-care professional asks, "On a scale of zero to ten, with ten being the most amount of pain you can imagine experiencing, what number would you choose to describe the pain you are now experiencing?"

Pain, we are told, is a subjective experience. We have a scale in the counseling profession called Subjective Units of Disturbance, or SUDS for short. When I ask a client to give a zero-to-ten rating on an event that may have happened many years ago, a considerable number will still rate the distress they experience about this event at least five or higher. As mentioned earlier, for some, even though the event happened thirty years ago or longer, the emotional and mental distress can be as fresh as if it happened yesterday.

How we perceive potential highly upsetting events, situations, or circumstances is subjective as well. I am still amazed when I hear stories where two people experience the same event, one seemed to walk away almost unscathed while the other reported feeling completely crushed and devastated by the same event. While there can be multiple explanations for this, the key here is to accurately assess and evaluate everyone's experience. This is an attempt to understand whether they believe or feel the event, situation, or circumstance was extremely upsetting or traumatic for them.

Often, in my experience, the treatment for trauma is different than most traditional theories and approaches to counseling. I decided to get additional training in a few approaches that have been found to be particularly effective in treating trauma. While there are other treatment modalities that have been demonstrated as helpful in addressing trauma, the two approaches I use the most in my practice and will describe in greater detail later are Eye Movement Desensitization and Reprocessing (EMDR) and Be Set Free Fast (BSFF).

For some single-instance traumatic events, these approaches can seem to be almost surgical through focusing exclusively on this one wounding experience. Counseling can still be very beneficial after this treatment intervention, especially to be able to address the distorted messages the individual began to believe about themselves, others, and God as a result of this wounding experience. Multiple instances of trauma can be more challenging and can take a longer period to heal substantially.

There is typically a focus on very specific events and then slicing those events carefully into manageable sections and many times pacing the work by carefully addressing one small section at time. Keep this in mind as I discuss various healing approaches later, as the noun form for "bind up" can be translated as "surgeon."

17

MOVING TOWARD A BETTER UNDERSTANDING OF THE SELF

Care requires understanding.

Dallas Willard

You shall love your neighbor as yourself.

Mark 12:31 NASB

A horrible command if the self were simply to be hated.

C. S. Lewis

David G. Benner said, "Leaving the self out of Christian spirituality results in a spirituality that is not well grounded in experience. It is, therefore, not well grounded in reality. Focusing on God while failing to know ourselves deeply may produce an external form of piety, but it will always leave a gap between appearance and reality. This is dangerous to the soul of anyone — and in spiritual leaders it can also be disastrous for those who lead."

I have discovered that many Christians seem to be quite conflicted over the concept of the self. Jesus was asked one day what the greatest commandment was. He replied, "Love the Lord your God with all your heart and with all your soul and with all your mind. This is the first and greatest commandment. And the second is like it: 'Love your neighbor as yourself.' All the Law and the Prophets hang on these two commandments" (Matthew 22:37–40 NIV).

I have run into quite a few Christians who are quite comfortable with the commands to "love God" and "love others" but get really uncomfortable with that whole "love yourself" thing. "It just seems so selfish and self-centered," they say.

It has always seemed quite clear to me that God is commanding us to love Him first and foremost (remember the order of things) and then love your neighbor as you love yourself. Isn't this what Jesus said? Some Christ followers like to say, "We need the full counsel of God here." Is leaving something out because we are uncomfortable with it or somehow think it is selfish really honoring "the full counsel of God"? The following quote from Bible scholars of the United Kingdom illustrates this:

> Where intensity and comprehensiveness mark a true love of God, parity is offered as the mark of true love of one's fellow human beings. Scholars have shown a great desire to find here an other-centredness that is self-disregarding: love of neighbour in place of love of self. But the wording hardly supports this. The text assumes positive self-regard and the care for oneself that goes with this, and therefore that behaving towards others as though one were oneself on the receiving end will produce kindly and considerate behaviour towards them. Self-disregard may be said to characterise love of God, but not love of neighbour. And since the two

commandments are coupled together, even love for God—that God who commands love of neighbour as oneself—should not be seen, despite all the rigours of discipleship, as extinguishing the significance of our own well-being (cf. Mt. 7:12; Eph. 5:29).[68]

All right, brothers and sisters, can I have an amen? A little louder?

"Therefore whatever you want others to do for you, do so for them, for this is the Law and the Prophets" (Matthew 7:12 NASB). "For no one ever hated his own flesh, but nourishes and cherishes it, just as Christ also does the church" (Ephesians 5:29 NASB).

Doesn't the Bible also say that the fleshly part of ourselves is bad, carnal, and sinful? The following verse certainly seems to indicate this. "For I know that nothing good dwells in me, that is, in my flesh; for the wishing is present in me, but the doing of the good is not" (Romans 7:18 NASB).

So, the use of the word *flesh* in Romans 7:18 seems to contradict its use and meaning in Ephesians 5:29. This is where we have to be careful with biblical interpretation. Some words, like *flesh*, have multiple shades of meaning in the original language. "Be diligent to present yourself approved to God as a workman who does not need to be ashamed, **handling accurately the word of truth** [emphasis added]" (2 Timothy 2:15 NASB).

W. E. Vine states, "Flesh (Greek, SARX) has a wider range of meaning in the New Testament than in the Old Testament." Here is a summary of his list of the following examples. I am including at least one of the passages he lists where this is the intended meaning:

- the substance of the body (1 Corinthians 15:39)
- the human body (Galatians 2:20)
- of mankind, in the totality of all that is essential to manhood (Matthew 24:22; John 1:13; Romans 3:20)

- **the holy humanity of the Lord Jesus, in the totality of all that is essential to manhood** [emphasis added] (John 1:14; 1 Timothy 3:16; 1 John 4:2)
- the complete person (John 6:51–57; James 5:3)
- the weaker element (Matthew 26:41; Romans 6:19)
- the unregenerate state (Romans 7:5, 8:8)
- the seat of sin (2 Peter 2:18; 1 John 2:16)
- the lower and temporary element (Galatians 3:3, 6:8)
- natural attainments (1 Corinthians 1:26)
- circumstances (1 Corinthians 7:28)
- the outward and seeming, as contrasted with the spirit, the inward and real (John 6:63; 2 Corinthians 5:16)
- natural relationship (1 Corinthians 10:18; Galatians 4:23)[69]

Willard clarifies some of the above-referenced definitions of the flesh. "This essential biblical term applies to the natural physical substance of a person, and it refers to the reservoir of finite independent powers inherent in the human body as a 'living being' among other living beings."[70]

In Christian theology, there is a clear distinction between the old self, which we are supposed to "die to," or "put off," and then "put on" the new self, who is being renovated. "Do not lie to each other, since you have taken off your old self with its practices and have put on the new self, which is being renewed in knowledge in the image of its Creator" (Colossians 3:9–10 NIV).

So, we need to be extremely careful whenever we see the terms *self* or *flesh* used in the Bible that we do not automatically assume that their use in a particular passage is automatically selfish, evil, wrong, or bad. If we do, we could be making a colossal mistake.

18
CHAPTER

DAMAGE, DECEPTION, DECISION, AND THE DISTORTED SELF

Research on the brain has discovered that the prefrontal cortex in boys and young men is not fully developed until their mid to late twenties. In young women, this complete development occurs somewhat earlier in their twenties.[71] This can offer at least a partial explanation why younger people can say and do some considerably unwise things.

Even though I could run fast, I was unfortunately unable to evade the following event. An incident occurred in middle school where I experienced a painful combination of betrayal and humiliation. Medical experts tell us that physical pain is a "subjective experience." Remember that medical experts tell us mental and emotional pain is no different. What may be a horrible experience for one person may barely phase another. Other less sensitive kids might have rolled with the punches on this day in middle school. Unfortunately, I did not. Suffice it to say, this event wounded me deeply. Only years later would I discover to what extent.

The following explanation of the impact of this experience is an adaptation of what I gleaned from listening to a CD set by John Eldredge called *The Four Streams*.[72]

- **The Damage:** Betrayal and Humiliation
- **The Deception:** "People can't be trusted."
- **The Decision:** "I'll never open myself up to another person again."

Due to damage and the subsequent deception I bought into, I distinctly remember making the decision to begin to close off parts of myself to others. On some level (subconsciously), I believe I was trying to prevent ever having to experience this gut-wrenching intensity of relational and emotional pain again.

- **The Distortion:** Super safe, shut down, silent Joe who keeps everything on the surface, opening up to no one.

When we get wounded (notice I do not say "if"), we are all capable of falling prey to this downward spiral of damage-deception-decision-distortion and then possibly becoming far less than we were intended to be. Remember all the many facets of our self that can be broken?

Now back to my own distorted self of "super safe, shut down, silent Joe." I was able to keep this internal promise through middle school up to the beginning of my senior year in high school. A friend and teammate on my high school football team prevailed on me to join the high school choir, and that experience began to soften my heart. That year I took the risk and began opening up to this friend. We also went to church together and were able to have open discussions about our lives, plus questions and issues that were at times faith related as well.

After college, we lost touch with one another for a good twenty years and reconnected through a curious series of events. Shortly afterwards, I received an email message, "Are you the Joe Arnold from Owenton, KY?"

I replied, "Yes, I am one and the same."

We actively reestablished our friendship and now get together on a regular basis for encouragement, support, and just having fun, with no secrets to this day.

Some who may read this who knew me in middle school and high school will think, *I had no idea any of this was going on.*

You wouldn't. We all become quite adept at concealing our internal wounds. Although I thought I felt somewhat safe in this distorted self that I formed, it was also a considerably lonely place. For me, athletics and academics were the arenas where I sought out and found worth and validation during my middle school, high school, and early college days. My family of origin, extended family, church family, growing personal faith, teachers, and coaches were anchors and places of refuge as well.

Someone has suggested that we need to be more compassionate with ourselves and those we encounter because we are either "going into a battle, in the midst of a battle, or coming out of a battle." While we are all grateful for times of relative ease, M. Scott Peck's assertion that "life is difficult"[73] is a reality that we all have to come to terms with.

I have not been able to completely elude this distorted self I became in my adolescence. I think, on some level, we are all trying to find ways to give our lives meaning and significance. Growing up in a family of achievers, I believed that if I did enough important stuff, this would automatically make me feel significant. As a result, I've attempted to work and push harder, but what I thought I was seeking always seemed to be just out of my grasp. All along I've wanted to somehow accomplish more things, but I sensed God was drawing me to be more real through finding my significance in Him.

We've probably all had the rich experience of sitting with someone who is listening intently to us, and then, all of the sudden, we have the realization, "Now here's someone who really seems to understand me!" Several years ago, I took Dallas Willard's book, *Hearing God: Developing a Conversational Relationship with God*, on a personal retreat to the monastery at St. Meinrad, Indiana. Over and over, I had the rich mystical experience of the deep longing to be known by God and another individual as I was pondering different aspects of a transformational interaction with my heavenly Father. I enjoyed this time immensely, reading, resting, and reflecting, and in one sense, it felt like I was sitting in the living room with Dallas Willard, with God's Holy Spirit being ever present as well.

Inside the book cover, I read where *Hearing God* was a part of a series by InterVarsity Press called "Formatio." At the close of the paragraph describing this series are the words, "We believe that each of us is made with a deep desire to be in God's presence. Formatio books help us to fulfill our deepest desires and become our true selves in the light of God's grace."

With this description of the Formatio *series,* I was gently confronted with the idea that I can be something less than my true self, lapsing into a false version of myself, far less than the real individual I was created to become. In a real-life dialogue with Dallas Willard, John Ortberg quotes him as saying,

The most important thing in your life is not what you do; it's who you become. That's what you will take into eternity. You are an unceasing spiritual being with an eternal destiny in God's great universe.

Brother John, you think you have to be someplace else or accomplish something more to find peace. But it's right here. God has yet to bless anyone except where they actually are.[74]

Do you have a deepening sense when you are drifting off to sleep at night that you are increasingly becoming your true self? Have you, like myself, lived for periods of your life not out of this true self, but from some false representation of the real you? As you read these last two sentences, could there be a part of you that feels strangely drawn to both affirm and discover more of your unique, true self?

Damage can lead to distortion, which can derail or detour our true destination.

19
CHAPTER

THE DISTORTED SELF

A number of other authors have weighed in, using different language, to attempt to more clearly identify and understand what I am calling The Distorted Self.

"Illusory person"—Thomas Merton
"The false superself"—David A. Seamands
"The Imposter"—Brenan Manning
"Masking"—Marita Littauer and Florence Littauer
"The false self"—John Eldredge

distort

- to twist out of the true meaning
- alter or pervert to give a false or unnatural picture or account
- to twist out of a natural, normal, or original shape or condition
- wrench into an unnatural shape or condition
- to twist or make misshapen mentally or morally
- "delusions of various kinds *distorted* his outlook on life . . ."[75]

Thomas Merton has said that the only member of God's creation that can choose to be something other than their true selves are human beings. Merton, originally from New York, spent years of his life as a monk at the Cistercian Abbey of Gethsemani, located in a beautiful part of central Kentucky.

I must confess at the outset that I am still very much on the journey of unmasking aspects of my false self and hopefully allowing a truer version of myself to continue to emerge. I've also learned through Brennan Manning's writings that the struggle with this far lesser image can be a battle we will contend with throughout our entire lives.

As I mentioned earlier, John Eldredge was the first writer/speaker to introduce to me the whole idea and possibility of the false self and what I have referred to as the distorted self. I am borrowing largely from other writers here by design because I have less experience wrestling with and unmasking the false self and intentionally living into a truer version of myself. To be honest, the whole idea that I could live this life and not really be my truest, most authentic self is troubling to me, to say the least.

A big part of the reason I am presenting this idea is to further my own dialogue with God, myself, and you, the reader. I have found some of Thomas Merton's writings to be particularly helpful in both understanding and recognizing this false self. Growing up in rural Kentucky and beholding some of the wonders of nature he writes about touches me in deeper places. Here is a sample of some of the fruit of Merton's contemplation in this area:

> The special clumsy beauty of this particular colt on this April day in this field under these clouds is a holiness consecrated to God by his own creative wisdom and it declares the glory of God.[76]

The pale flowers of the Dogwood outside this window are saints. The little yellow flowers that nobody notices on the edge of that road are Saints looking up into the face of God.[77]

This leaf has its own texture and its own pattern of veins and its own holy shape, and the bass and trout hiding in the deep pools of the river are canonized by their beauty and their strength.

The lakes hidden among the hills are saints, and the sea too is a saint who praises God without interruption in her majestic dance.[78]

Merton continues,

For me to be a saint means to be myself. Therefore the problem of sanctity and salvation is in fact the problem of finding out who I am and of discovering my true self.[79]

Trees and animals have no problem. God makes them what they are without consulting them, and they're perfectly satisfied.

With us it is different. God leaves us free to be whatever we like. We can be ourselves or not, as we please. We are at liberty to be real, or to be unreal. We may be true or false, the choice is ours. We may wear now one mask and now another, and never, if we so desire, appear with our own true face. But we cannot make these choices without impunity. Causes have effects, and if we lie to ourselves and others, then we cannot expect to find truth and reality whenever we happen to want them. If we have chosen the way of falsity we must not be surprised that truth eludes us when we finally come to need it.[80]

Every one of us is shadowed by an illusory person: a false self.

This is the person that I want myself to be but who cannot exist, because God does not know anything about him. And to be unknown to God is altogether too much privacy.

My false and private self is the one who wants to exist outside the reach of God's will and God's love - outside of reality and outside of life. And such a self cannot help but be an illusion.

We are not very good at recognizing illusions, least of all the ones we cherish about ourselves—the ones we are born with and which feed the roots of sin. For most of the people in the world, there is no greater subjective reality than this false self of theirs, which cannot exist. A life devoted to the cult of this shadow is what is called a life of sin.[81]

All sins starts from the assumption that my false self, the self that exists only in my own egocentric desires, is the fundamental reality of life to which everything else in the universe is ordered. Thus I use up my life in the desire for pleasures and the thirst for experiences, for power, honor, knowledge and love, to clothe this false self and construct its nothingness into something objectively real.[82]

I have read and reread the following quotes from Merton numerous times, and I continue to ponder the meaning of what he has written for myself and those I care for. Merton's conceptualizations of the false self-resonate with a solid ring of truth for me.

If this is so, the false self is unable to make deep transformational change because it is not real. I believe the hope for this type of change occurs when we can take an honest and earnest look at ourselves: our wounds, our moral failures/values violations, the subsequent distortions of ourselves, and a willingness to seek the truth at any cost. Could it be possible that we are both knowingly and unknowingly hiding from reality?

Over some time as I have reflected on Merton's words, one of my false selves that I have struggled with is "the smart guy." This really goes way back for me. At some point in my elementary school years, I took a black felt-tipped permanent marker and wrote on the door of a white metal storage cabinet in our garage, "Joe is called the brain."

My Mom said when I was a little fellow, I said to her, "When I grow up, I'm going to be a *buffessor*." While I never achieved this standing in an academic setting, I think the fellow who uttered this statement as a small child thought of himself as a quite intelligent little guy.

My early academic success affirmed this belief in myself. This "smart guy" identity that I was forming met its first challenge in the eighth grade. My English/literature teacher gave me my first C on my report card. I was crushed!

I still to this day remember her telling me, "Joe Arnold, you are going to make some C's."

To which, my insides wanted to shout, "Say it isn't so!"

This statement to me wound up being quite prophetic, as I made several more C's on my report card during the course of my academic career.

It pains me to admit this, but this false self has crept into my career at times as a professional counselor, and I'm confident in other settings as well. Sometimes this illusory self can get hooked by a simple question posed to me by a client. Suddenly, instead of the primary focus being serving my client with the gifts God has cultivated in me, "the smart guy" can creep in and whisper, "Impress them with your knowledge! Dazzle them with your brilliance!"

If I cave to this—and I must admit I have on many occasions—the session focus suddenly shifts from being all about them to being all about me.

I want to be very clear at this point that there is nothing wrong with perceiving yourself as smart or intelligent. Being somewhat intelligent can be a good thing and a considerable gift. But remember, this is only a single dimension of who we really are. Timothy Keller warns us about making a good thing an *ultimate* thing. I believe there is a strong temptation in all of humanity to move toward idolizing or worshiping the gift or gifts, making them the foundation or the central organizing principle of our lives.

Gifts or dimensions of our lives were never intended to bear the full weight of our existence. Rejoice and be grateful for the gifts you may have. But beware of the trap of creating a false self solely on these gifts and leaving the path of humble dependence on the Giver of all these good gifts.

"Every good and perfect gift is from above, coming down from the Father of heavenly lights, who does not change like shifting shadows" (James 1:17 NIV). Thomas Merton wrote, "The secret of my identity is hidden in the love and mercy of God."

I've had a longing to be more real, genuine, or authentic—whichever word you want to use—for about as long as I can remember. It is also so easy to attempt to define ourselves solely by the current roles or responsibilities we have.

Here is a list of some of my vocational identities: youth minister, student-athlete, middle and high school teacher and coach, college assistant football coach and residence hall director, targeted assessment specialist, husband, stepparent, step grandparent, licensed professional clinical counselor, board-certified coach, and certified brain health coach (by the Amen Clinic). I've probably left off a few other hats I have worn over the years. I'm discovering that my true self far and away transcends all the career and vocational choices and the various roles and responsibilities we take on.

The first step in our pilgrimage of discovering our true selves is recognizing there is a God, and we are his creatures. As human beings, we are the only creatures distinctly created in His own image. We are the apex of His creation. In a Vacation Bible School (VBS) I attended as a child, one summer we memorized Psalm 100 (KJV).

> Make a joyful noise unto the Lord, all ye lands. Serve the Lord with gladness, Come before His presence with singing. Know ye that the Lord, He is God. It is He that hath made us, and not we ourselves. We are His people and the sheep of his pasture. Enter into His gates with thanksgiving, And into His courts with praise. Be thankful unto Him, and bless His name. For the Lord is good. His mercy is everlasting, And His truth endureth to all generations.

After all these years, I was (almost) able to quote this from memory! Many thanks to my childhood VBS director of days gone by, Mary Kinney Shipp!

Want more? Check out these resources:
Thomas Merton, *New Seeds of Contemplation*

David G. Benner, *The Gift of Being Yourself*

Brennan Manning with Jim Hancock, *Posers, Fakers, and Wannabes (Unmasking the Real You)*

20
CHAPTER

THE UNQUENCHABLE
THIRST OF THE FALSE SELF

*"For My people have committed two evils: They have
forsaken Me, the fountain of living waters, to hew for
themselves cisterns, broken cisterns, that can hold no water"*

(Jeremiah 2:13 NASB).

When we set out on a path to get our own perceived needs met
and fashion our own self, apart from reliance on God, we empower
a false self. As a result, when left exclusively to our own devices
(no technology pun intended), we can become desperate and
demanding at times in our digging expeditions to find what we then
perceive to be crucial for our life, like the necessity of water.

As we move toward and live into the false self and depend on
our broken cisterns, we can experience a gnawing hunger and
discontent. Something is amiss. When our attempts to find life
away from God do not deeply satisfy, we can turn to a host of

compensatory strategies to address the ache within. We can seek distractions for the ache, try to numb it, avoid it through some form of denial, or demand that someone or something soothe it. Some try to assuage the pain with more activity or another distraction. Others reach a place of resignation where they just give up trying altogether. The appetite of the false self is insatiable.

But David penned these words about God in a song, "who satisfies your desires with good things so that your youth is renewed like the eagle's."[83]

Then there's the famous story of Jesus with the woman at the well.

> Jesus answered her, "If you knew the gift of God and who it is that asks you for a drink, you would have asked him and he would have given you living water". "Sir", the woman said, "you have nothing to draw with and the well is deep. Where can you get this living water? Are you greater than our father Jacob, who gave us the well and drank from it himself, as did also his sons, his flocks and herds?" Jesus answered, "Everyone who drinks this water will be thirsty again, but whoever drinks the water I give him will never thirst. Indeed, the water I give him will become in him a spring of water welling up to eternal life."[84]

When we bring our true, broken selves to God, He is able to substantially satisfy our true thirst. The thirst of the false self will never be satisfied and will continually struggle to find genuine contentment because it will never bow in humble dependence upon God.

21
CHAPTER

THE TRUE SELF

Due to being created in the very image of God, we have incredible potential for goodness, if not greatness. Could it be that or longing for perfection hearkens back to a time earlier in the garden of Eden when the first man and woman were perfect, before the Fall? Lewis B. Smedes said, "A healthy sense of shame is perhaps the surest sign of our divine origin and our human dignity. We know it by a deep intuition we have of the better person we would be if we truly were all we could be."

Benner says the true self is "your total self as you were created by God and as you are being redeemed in Christ. It is the image of God that you are—the unique face of God that has been set aside for eternity for you."[85] Benner continues, "We do not find our true self by seeking it. Rather, we find it by seeking God ... in finding God, we find our truest and deepest self."[86]

Benner presents a chart, where he compares and contrasts the false self with the true self. There are two aspects on his chart that are particularly meaningful to me at this juncture in my understanding of my own true self.

I have been a performance-oriented and activity/task-driven person most of my life. If I simply carry over this propensity in my relationship with God, everything will feel performance driven to the point of exhaustion, and old perfectionistic attitudes resurface of "I can never quite do enough to please God or to feel completely accepted by Him." This is the trap of my false perfectionistic self.

It is with great relief that I embrace these aspects of the true self!

False Self	True Self
Achieved by means of pretense and practice	Received as a gift with gratitude and surrender
Maintained by effort and control	Maintained by grace[87]

To be able to receive my true self first and foremost as a gift from God is liberating for me beyond what words can express. While this is initially received as a gift, understanding and increasingly living into of this true self is the ongoing journey of a lifetime. The temptation is always there to live and operate far beneath our true self.

To offer clarity about effort, Dallas Willard said, "God is not opposed to effort, He is opposed to earning."

I believe the key to balance here is the concept of stewardship. Stewardship is the idea of taking care of, developing, and even attempting to optimize the gifts and abilities that we have been given. The possibility of considerable creative potential is present in these gifts and abilities, but unless we harness and develop them, they will always just be potential, but not concrete reality. This is the place where we can truly bless the world in which we live with how we have been blessed.

Every human being is endowed with certain temperamental qualities, gifts, and abilities and may have an affinity to develop and grow specific talents and areas of interest. Everyone is also unique with a unique DNA. No one else will be able to express God's grace, goodness, and creativity in the exact manner that you can.

Someone has said, "Our life is a gift from God. What we do with it is our gift back to God." One tool for greater self-understanding, to help you move down the pathway of beginning to know yourself as you truly are, is the Enneagram. The Enneagram has intrigued me for years, but I have allowed one thing or another to prevent me from exploring the riches of this tool in depth for me. As a result, I must confess that I am only in the nursery school of understanding myself here.

I have found David G. Benner's book listed below to be a great help in navigating through our false selves to a truer version of who we are.

Want more? Check out these resources:
The Gift of Being Yourself by David G. Benner.

The Road Back to You by Ian Morgan Cron and Suzanne Stabile

22
CHAPTER

INNER MAN OR INNER BEING

"I pray that out of his glorious riches he may strengthen you with power through his Spirit **in your inner being** *[emphasis added]"*

(Ephesians 3:16 NIV).

"For in my inner being I delight in God's law"

(Romans 7:22 NIV).

"For this reason, I bow my knees before the Father, from whom every family in heaven and earth derives its name, that He would grant you, according to the riches of his glory, to be strengthened with power thorough His Spirit **in the inner man***; so that Christ may dwell in your hearts through faith; and that you, being rooted and grounded in love, may be able to comprehend with all the saints what is the breadth and length and height and depth, and to know the love of Christ which surpasses knowledge, that you may be filled up to all the fullness of God [emphasis added]"*

(Ephesians 3:14–19 NASB).

This section was my attempt to answer some questions for myself. What is this inner being? Is it the new self that the apostle Paul speaks of? Is the new self a part of the true self or vice versa? Are they one in the same? Here is a little bit of what I discovered from some respected sources of biblical scholarship.

So how is the inner man/being defined?

> the spiritual side of man, or man himself in so far as he enjoys self-awareness, as he thinks and wills and feels. As such, as the subject of the power of moral judgment, he is accessible to the divine revelation, can be conditioned by it and is open to its claim
>
> In the petition in Eph. 3:16, the term is also to be understood of man as the object of God's working or of the place in man at which the power of the Spirit meets and determines him.
>
> As used by Paul, the word always carries with it a suggestion, like the parallel in 1 Pt. 3:4, of something which is concealed, and which works in concealment, in the innermost part of man.[88]

And . . .

> The "inner self" is the whole person as a "new creation" (2 Corinthians 5:17) or a "new person" (Colossians 3:9–10), "the renewed being of the Christian," the spiritual aspect of the believer.[89]

Leanne Payne discussed praying with someone for "the strengthening of their will," and I originally found this a little odd.

I have received some training in the chemical dependency field and exposure to AA literature. Just applying more willpower *is* the problem. What if this willpower is coming from the old self that we need to die to?

It seems to me that to pray for the will to be strengthened, this would be "the spiritual side" of the Christ follower that "thinks, wills, and feels." What if this is the place where true transformation of our true selves takes place? What if whatever is in this innermost part is really what is largely controlling us? What if this is what some have called either the subconscious or now being called in some circles the nonconscious metacognitive mind?

> God has designed the brain in such a way that the intrinsic activity in the nonconscious part of our minds is where most of the mind action takes place, **and it is always dominant twenty-four hours a day**. It is where we are thinking, choosing, building, and sorting thoughts. Simply put, it is the constant, high-energy activity that is always going on in the nonconscious mind, even when we are resting. **What we consciously think and what we say and do is all driven by information and activity in the nonconscious mind** [emphasis added].[90]

If this is true, do you think some of the focus of our interventions need to seriously consider this cognitive nonconscious dimension? This will be explored further in a chapter on BSFF.

"To be made new in the attitude of your minds; and to put on **the new self**, created to be like God in true righteousness and holiness [emphasis added]" (Ephesians 4:23–24 NIV).

SOME PATHWAYS TOWARD THE HEALING OF BROKENNESS

23

HEALING BROKENNESS EXPLORED FURTHER

What if some substantial brokenness, for some, is healed at the time of Christian conversion?

In a recent newsletter from the Billy Graham Evangelistic Association, an eighteen-year-old young lady made a commitment of her life to Christ, joined a choir, started reading her Bible, and participated in an online discipleship course. She stated, "My life is better now with Jesus ... I am no longer broken and hurt, but whole and at peace."[91]

I do not question for a second that an all-powerful God is more than able to heal much of our brokenness either during or shortly after conversion. After my recommitment to Christ at age nineteen, I believe some broken parts of my own heart were healed. But what I've discovered in my own journey is that there were more broken places to be healed in my life, as I became aware of them. As the years have gone by, I've learned about some other pathways toward healing I was previously unaware of as well.

Professor and pastoral minister David Seamands offers his experienced perspective on this issue.

> A great crisis experience of Jesus Christ, as important and eternally valuable as this is, is not a shortcut to emotional health. It is not a quickie cure for personality problems.
>
> It is necessary that we understand this, first of all, so we can compassionately live with ourselves and allow the Holy Spirit to work with special healing in our own hurts and confusions. We also need to understand this in order to not judge other people too harshly, but to have patience with their confusing and contradictory behavior. In doing so, we will be kept from unfairly criticizing and judging other Christians. They're not fakes, phonies, or hypocrites. They are people, like you and me, with **hurts and scars and wrong programming** that interfere with their present behavior [emphasis added].[92]

Even if God were able to heal our hearts completely, at the moment of conversion, what about other troubling or traumatic events that may occur after becoming a Christ follower? What if wounding experiences begin to surface that have been buried for years? Flashbacks begin? A diagnosis of PTSD?

The example of Simon Peter, who later became the apostle Peter, is illustrative here. Even though his approach seemed impulsive at times, few, if any, would question his sincerity as a Christ follower. Jesus issued this warning to Peter, "Simon, Simon, Satan has asked to sift you as wheat. But I have prayed for you, Simon, that your faith may not fail. And when you have turned back, strengthen your brothers."[93]

After Peter's three betrayals of Jesus Christ prior to his crucifixion, I believe that Peter perceived himself as broken and "completely washed up" as a follower of Christ. It's no surprise that he returned to his previous vocation of fishing.

In order to restore this disciple, Jesus made a post-resurrection appearance to Peter and made a point to engage him both specifically and individually. Peter deeply wounded himself in the betrayals, and in this damaged state, he no longer saw himself as worthy to be a disciple. I am convinced that Peter needed more than just forgiveness from his Lord and Savior. He needed divine encouragement and Jesus's ministry of "binding up the brokenhearted," personally experiencing His healing hand of restoration.[94]

Is it possible that Peter remembered Jesus's words from the verses listed above when you have turned back and wondered, "Could this really be another chance for me?" I believe Peter embraced this moment and received the healing and restoration he desperately needed. For evidence of the change, just read the book of Acts.

The same resurrected Jesus, though not now visible in bodily form, is still in the business of healing and restoring our broken selves today.

24
CHAPTER

CAN SOME TYPES OF BROKENNESS BE A GOOD THING?

"My sacrifice, O God, is a broken spirit; a broken and contrite heart you, God, will not despise"

(Psalm 51:17 NIV).

There is clearly a form or type of brokenness, referenced here by the psalmist, which is not harmful to our heart or destructive to our true selves. Elsewhere in James 4:6–10 (NASB), we find these words:

But He gives greater grace. Therefore it says, "God is opposed to the proud, but gives grace to the humble". Submit therefore to God, resist the Devil, and he will flee from you. Draw near to God, and He will draw near to you. Cleanse your hands, you sinners; purify your hearts, you double-minded. Be miserable and mourn and weep; let your laughter be turned to mourning, and your joy to gloom. Humble yourselves in the presence of the Lord, and He will exalt you.

Sorrow is a sacred thing.

William Cowper

There is an experience of godly sorrow that can be good for us all.

> Even if I caused you sorrow by my letter, I do not regret
> it. Though I did regret it—I see that my letter hurt you,
> but only for a little while—yet now I am happy, not
> because you were made sorry, but because your sorrow
> led you to repentance. For you became sorrowful as
> God intended and so were not harmed any way by us.
> Godly sorrow brings repentance that leads to salvation
> and leaves no regret, but worldly sorrow brings death. (2
> Corinthians 7:8–10 NIV)

Being broken in this manner, accompanied with appropriate godly
sorrow, would absolutely be a *good thing*. We need to pray that the
Holy Spirit does his convicting work in these areas. There may be a
role for us to play in this process. "Brothers, if someone is caught
in a sin, you who are spiritual should restore him gently. But watch
yourself, or you may also be tempted" (Galatians 6:1 NIV).

Continue to pray, encourage, and set appropriate limits when
necessary. But do not attempt to play the role of the Holy Spirit.

GRACE ENCOUNTER: SUNLIGHT AND RAINDROP REFRESHMENT

"For he gives his sunlight to both the evil and the good, and he sends the rain on the just and the unjust alike"

(Matthew 5:45b NLT).

In *Common Grace*, Timothy Keller writes, "The Bible consistently teaches what theologians have come to call "common grace," a non-saving grace that is at work in the broader reaches of human cultural interaction. This gift of God's grace to humanity in general demonstrates a desire on God's part to bestow certain blessings on all human beings, believer and non-believer alike."

We ALL receive this.

Many don't fully see it or recognize it.

they did not honor him as God or give thanks ...[95]

> Some of these aspects of healing will descend on us like
> "filtered flickering sunlight" or "sprinkles of rain".
>
> There is a certain daily-ness about this as well for the
> apprentice of Christ ...

> It comes the very moment you wake up each morning.
> All your wishes and hopes for the day rush at you like
> wild animals. And the first job each morning consists
> simply in shoving them all back; in listening to that other
> voice, taking that other point of view, letting that other
> larger, stronger, quieter life come flowing in. And so on,
> all day. Standing back from all your natural fussings and
> frettings; coming in out of the wind. (C. S. Lewis, *Mere
> Christianity*)

"The Lord's loving kindnesses indeed never cease, for His
compassions never fail. They are new every morning, great is Thy
faithfulness" (Lamentations 3:22–23 NASB). "Therefore we do not
lose heart, but though our outer man is decaying, yet our inner
man is being renewed day by day" (2 Corinthians 4:16 NASB).

25

A CLOSER LOOK AT THE DEFINITION OF "BIND UP"

*He has sent me to **bind up** the brokenhearted . . .*

(Isaiah 61:1)

שָׁבַח (ḥā·ḇǎš): verb

Encourage, formally, bind up, that is, speak words which hearten and enliven one's feelings and attitudes, as a figurative extension of bandaging up a wound (Isaiah 61:1+)

שֹׁבֵחַ (ḥō·ḇēš): noun

remedy, that is, medicine or procedures which promote healing (Isaiah 3:7+); note: some translate as "surgeon," as one who binds wounds and heals

English translation, *healer*[96]

125

... speak words ...

"The thief comes only to steal, and kill, and destroy; I came that they might have life and have it abundantly" (John 10:10 NASB).

> *"The tongue that brings healing is a tree of life, but a deceitful tongue crushes the spirit"*
>
> (Proverbs 15:4 NIV).

Take a moment and reread, at least a couple of times, Proverbs 15:4 written above. Allow the profound impact of words to wash over you. It seems crystal clear that words spoken by our tongue have the potential to provide considerable healing or completely devastate us. There is a profound depth and richness here that I can only scratch the surface. I feel compelled to commend the writings Dallas Willard in this area.[97]

Here is where he ponders some of these questions:

- How is it that words have such a power to affect reality?
- Is it through their relationship to personality?
- What is that relationship?
- In what way are words a spiritual force?

... speak words which hearten *internally* ...

"Surely you desire truth in the inner parts; you teach me wisdom in the inmost place" (Psalm 51:6 NIV).

"Therefore we do not lose heart, but though our outer man is decaying, yet our inner man is being renewed day by day" (2 Corinthians 4:16 NASB).

What if what is in the "inner parts" or "inmost place" of our lives is not true about us, others, God, and the world in which we live? If that is the case, then how do we get what is true in these "inner parts"?

There is God's part in this process, but there is clearly a part we play as well. This is one of many paradoxical truths in the Bible.

26
CHAPTER

LUKE'S DIMENSIONS OF GROWTH AND HEALING

We know very little about the life of Jesus between the age of twelve and thirty. Luke the physician gives us a profoundly rich, multifaceted window of growth in a single, solitary statement describing this time period. "And Jesus kept increasing in wisdom and stature, and in favor with God and men" (Luke 2:52 NASB).

Four very important dimensions where Jesus "kept increasing" include the following:

- "wisdom"—mental/emotional/psychological dimension
- "stature"—physical/biological dimension
- "favor with God"—spiritual dimension
- "favor with men"—social dimension

These four areas will serve as the basic, but not exhaustive or exclusive, dimensions in the healing of our brokenness. These dimensions are in no way unique, but in some way, I am amazed at how a physician (Luke) several thousand years ago recognized the crucial importance of *growing in*, and I would add the possibility of *healing in*, all these areas. The four areas are also not mutually exclusive of one another, and a positive intervention in one area will almost invariably have a positive spillover effect in all the other areas. The converse is also true.

Is the order in which Luke lists these dimensions significant? As mentioned in the previous chapter, is it possible that there could be a divine order of approaching these areas? I absolutely believe there is, and some evidence from the scientific community seems to be bearing this out.

Consider the following. Is Luke 2:52 a divine order for growth and healing?

Wisdom (Mental/Psychological)

"The application is for all walks of life. You won't forgive that person, get rid of that anxiety or depression, follow that essential preventive healthcare, strive to that intellectual level you know you are capable of, follow that dream, eat that organic food, do that diet, be that great parent or husband or wife or friend, get that promotion, or make other changes to create a positive quality lifestyle-*unless you first choose to get your mind right and switch on your brain.* After all, the ability to think and choose and to use your mind correctly is often the hardest step, but it is the first and most powerful step."[98]

Awareness is critical.

Recognition that we might be broken.

Open to the possibility and apprehension of grace.

We must first decide here to be concerned enough to care about the other three areas.

I keep asking that the God of our Lord Jesus Christ, the glorious Father, may give you the spirit of wisdom and revelation so you may know Him better. I pray also that the eyes of your heart may be enlightened so you may know the hope to which He has called you, the riches of His glorious inheritance in the saints (Ephesians 1:17–18 NIV).

Stature (Physical/Biological)

Trying to help some patients change without first fixing their brain imbalances is like trying to get software to work on a computer whose hard drive is faulty.[99]

"The lamp of the body is the eye; if therefore your eye is clear, your whole body will be full of light" (Matthew 6:22 NASB).

David G. Benner writes, "Spiritual transformation involves the purification of sight … We have to learn to see—and accept—what is really there."

Overall brain/body health is critical here to be able to see clearly. For me, this included the understanding of some temperament dimensions: sensitivity (high/low), introversion/extroversion, and pursuit of excellence/perfectionism. If you are exhausted, distracted, sick, self-absorbed, have a brain injury or imbalance, or are in significant pain, you have far fewer resources and energy available to pursue either spiritual or social growth.

Favor with God (Spiritual)

"He has made everything beautiful in its time. He has also set eternity in the human heart; yet no one can fathom what God has done from the beginning to the end" (Ecclesiastes 3:11 NIV).

Even though we cannot fully fathom the eternal, if the heart that God set in us shattered, could this cause us to struggle in areas He desperately wants us to have the capability to respond?

"For God so loved the world that he gave his one and only Son, that whoever believes in him shall not perish but have eternal life" (John 3:16 NIV).

What if substantial healing of mind and body of our shattered self can enable greater capacity for enhanced spiritual experience?

Favor with Men (Social)

With this more substantially healed and whole self, I am now more able and ready to love God more completely with all my heart, soul, strength, and mind.[100] I am also more fully able to experience favor with man and enter into healthier relationships with yourself and others. "Love your neighbor as you love yourself."[101]

It is my contention that this divine order really does matter. If this really is the case, then being able to see clearly (the wisdom/mental/psychological dimension) and understand ourselves, others, God, and our world is critically and primarily important. Remember, "The lamp of the body is the eye, if therefore your eye is clear, your whole body will be full of light" (Matthew 6:22 NASB).

27

CHAPTER

PRAYER OF INVOCATION

As mentioned earlier, I attended a Baptist church in my childhood and adolescence. Each Sunday morning, when you walked into the worship service, you would receive a bulletin from one of the ushers that contained the "order of service" for that particular day. At or near the beginning of each service, someone was selected, or volunteered, to officially open the worship service with the invocation.

This was an audacious prayer, where we believed through humbly asking God to be present in this worship service, that He would somehow actually mystically show up in all the various aspects of service. If Jesus is not only the Savior of our souls, but our ultimate healer as well, then it seems His presence is desperately needed in the healing of our broken selves.

I read later where Leanne Payne, John Eldredge, and others were employing this same invocation prayer in their work with others in the healing of their brokenness. So, I have reclaimed some of my Baptist heritage through using forms of invocation prayer with consenting counselees who identify themselves as Christ followers. It is sometimes as simple as this prayer used by John Eldredge,

"Jesus, I invite you into this broken place within me (this wound, this memory)."[102]

Some, like myself, may be a bit fearful to open up and delve into these broken places. Leanne Payne also prays for the Lord to only reveal what the individual is "able to bear" in this specific instance at this particular time.

After this invocation prayer, different healing approaches may be used, tailored to the specific needs or wounding experiences of each individual client. Here is but a sampling from various authors and approaches of Jesus Christ being brought to bear to broken places:

- *Healing for Damaged Emotions* and *Healing of Memories* by David A. Seamands
- *The Healing Presence* and *Restoring the Christian Soul* by Leanne Payne
- www.wildatheart.org or the Wild at Heart app, "Prayers We Pray"
- Siang Yang Tan, "Inner Healing"[103]

These approaches that may be considered in a professional counseling context are required to have full, informed consent of the client. They are options for Christ followers who desire to take a more decidedly spiritual approach toward healing their brokenness.

Please note: Just because I have suggested these resources, this does not necessarily mean that I agree with everything each of these authors write about. I have been able to benefit from many books and resources from a variety of people that I may not agree with in every area that they teach and discuss.

GRACE ENCOUNTER: SLEEP

*In vain you rise early and stay up late, toiling for food
to eat – for he grants sleep to those he loves.*

Psalm 127:2 (NIV)

"Tomorrow is Saturday. Don't set any alarms. Sleep in."

My Dad came back to our bedroom and said this to my brother and
I quite often as we were growing up. I think I know now why he
enjoyed offering this rich privilege to my brother and me. Dad told
us that he and his older brother, Lee, would get up at five o'clock
every morning to go out and milk the cows before they would go to
school. I have the sense that getting to sleep in on a Saturday was
a rare treat, if ever, for my Dad when he was growing up. Except in
the summers, we got up early for school, Monday through Friday,
and we got up for Sunday school and church on Sundays. Saturday
then was the only real opportunity to sleep in, and I relished it.

As a nation, we sleep less today than any other time in recorded
history. "Research has shown a link between poor sleep habits and
sleep apnea, heart disease, high blood pressure, diabetes, and even
strokes."[104] "Bad sleeping habits in either children or parents can
have a devastating effect on the spiritual, emotional, and physical
health of the whole family."[105] Trying to drive a car when you are
sleepy is risky business. It is only by the grace of God that I have

not had a couple of bad accidents drifting off to sleep at the wheel when traveling by myself.

I began losing sleep in college, and I have struggled and battled with getting enough sleep my entire adult life. For me, and I believe many others, there always seems to be an endless list of things to do. I'm one of those people who has said for years, "There's just not enough time in a day to get everything done!" I've tried to squeeze more out of the day by sleeping less, and I have paid a considerable price. Years of not getting enough sleep began to diminish the quality of my life. I am absolutely a better version of myself when I am well rested.

When I'm not well rested, I get discouraged much more easily and struggle to be fully present with others. I have difficulty thinking clearly and overall have less to offer to my family and friends, plus the counseling clients whom I am attempting to serve.

To be able to get good sleep is a gift. I am convinced that we cannot consistently rob ourselves of sleep. There will always be a price to pay somewhere. For me, not getting enough sleep has eroded my experience of optimal health and well-being.

28

SELF ACCEPTANCE

Richard Lovelace writes in *Dynamics of Spiritual Life: An Evangelical Theology of Renewal*, "No realistic human beings find it easy to love or to forgive themselves, and hence their self-acceptance must be grounded in their awareness that God accepts them in Christ. There is a sense in which the strongest self–love that we can have, in the sense of agape, is merely the mirror image of the lively conviction we have that God loves us."

I can't remember how I first heard of the work and writings of Leanne Payne, but I will be forever grateful that I did. I was somewhat stunned to read the title of the second chapter of her book, *Restoring the Christian Soul*: "First Great Barrier to Wholeness in Christ: Failure to Accept Oneself"[106]

What? Why had I never read or heard this discussed in almost thirty years in all the Christian circles I'd been a part of? No one I knew of addressed the issue of self-acceptance as such a critical piece in our healing journey with Christ. I can only say it struck a chord that resonated deeply within me. Leanne Payne also referred to this as "The Great Christian Virtue of Self Acceptance."

In Matthew 16, Jesus began to tell his disciples that he must "go to Jerusalem, and suffer many things from the elders and chief priests and scribes, and be killed, and be raised up on the third day."[107] Later on in this discussion, he said to his disciples,

> If anyone wishes to be a follower of mine, he must leave self behind; he must take up his cross and come with me. Whoever cares for his own safety is lost; but if a man will let himself be lost for my sake, he will find his true self. What will a man gain by winning the whole world at the cost of his true self? Or what can he give that will buy that self back?[108]

Leanne Payne differentiates and explains this better than anyone else I have read up to this point in my life.

> A person may not accept himself when he is very self-centered, selfish, and has not died to the old self.
>
> He experiences real guilt, and it is a good thing that he is sorely afflicted with it. He cannot say with St. Paul and the Christian: "For we know that our old self was crucified with Him so the body of sin might be done away with, that we should no longer be slaves to sin" (Romans 6:6).
>
> It is therefore a mercy that he heartily dislikes and fails to accept that self, that he has honest negative thoughts about himself. But we must differentiate between the self that collaborates with the principle of evil and selfishness, and the self that abides in Christ and collaborates with him. That is the true self. That is the justified new creation, the soul that is saved and lives

eternally. The former self we deliberately and continually die to; the other we joyfully and in great humility and thankfulness accept.

But it is only with the full acceptance of this new self that we find our true center, that place of quiet strength and solid being [emphasis added].[109]

Payne continues, "The humble acceptance of myself as fallen but now justified by Another who is my righteousness is the basis on which I can accept myself, learn to laugh at myself, be patient with myself."[110]

There is so much more Leanne Payne has to say about the value of this self-acceptance, and I commend to you her writings in this area. For many, Payne would say that movement toward a healthy self- acceptance is a journey as opposed to a singular healing event.

It will truly be to our own detriment if we try to disregard or bypass this healthy self-acceptance out of some concern that we are being selfish for attempting to know and understand ourselves better. You may be surprised to find out how some saints of yesteryear viewed God and the self:

- "Grant, Lord, that I may know myself that I may know thee" (Augustine).
- "Nearly the whole of sacred doctrine consists in these two parts: knowledge of God and of ourselves" (John Calvin, *Institutes of the Christian Religion*, 1536).

29
CHAPTER

PRAYER FOR RENUNCIATION
OF SELF HATRED?

Brennan Manning, author of *A Glimpse of Jesus: The Stranger to Self-Hatred*, writes, "Self-hatred is the predominant spiritual problem that I've had to deal with in twenty-eight years as a vagabond evangelist."

I've struggled with aspects of self-acceptance, in one way or another, most of my life. Was it really true that I could possibly pray a prayer and begin to move toward a more authentic experience of this "great virtue" Payne spoke of? I have since learned that some may have to pray this prayer several times to obtain more substantial relief in this area. Back then, I was ready to go to whatever lengths necessary to experience more freedom and true acceptance in this area.

This prayer she recommended was called the "Prayer of Renunciation of Self Hatred."[111] This at first sounded a little too strong for me. I was aware that I disliked certain aspects of myself, for example, parts of my physical appearance, but did I really hate these aspects of myself? Some of my clients over the years assured me that the terms *self-loathing* and *self-hatred* were definitely not too strong for them in their own struggle for self-acceptance. My desire for release and the potential for greater healing prevailed. I decided to pray this prayer verbatim, out loud, the next time I had some free moments of solitude.

I can still remember the night that I decided to pray this prayer. I was alone at home, and it seemed like a good opportunity. I literally prayed the prayer out loud in good faith. I felt calm after the prayer, but nothing dramatic happened. It was while I was getting ready the next morning that I began to notice a difference. I looked at myself in the mirror and just walked away, with no negative thoughts or self-accusations going on in my mind against my appearance. This destructive, self-talk about my appearance when I looked in a mirror is largely gone, and the pattern of internal bashing of myself has also largely ceased.

Payne is careful to say that not everyone experiences this same release the first time they pray this prayer. Continuing to pray this prayer for a season plus counseling may be needful and necessary for some to break through to more freedom in this area.

I have also read portions of Brennan Manning's book, *A Glimpse of Jesus*, which I quoted from at the beginning of this section. I can easily recommend this as a potential healing resource if you have wrestled in your own journey with feelings of self-loathing and self-hatred.

Are you willing to do whatever it takes to be a more healed, whole person? General Naaman had to dip in the dirty Jordan River seven times to receive his healing from leprosy.

GRACE ENCOUNTER: WONDER

"Whether the morning and evening of one day or of many days had passed Frodo could not tell. He did not feel either hungry or tired, only filled with wonder. The stars shone through the window and the silence of the heavens seemed to be round him."

J. R. R. Tolkien, *The Lord of the Rings*,
(New York: Ballantine Books, 1954-1974)

I was eating supper with my Dad in a gambling casino (we were wild men). In a rare moment while we were sharing supper together, he began to describe an experience when he was in the Army Dental Corp after World War II, I believe while stationed in France, during the European occupation. His eyes and his face began to light up as he described several events over the course of being out one evening ... the lights ... the colors ... He looked off into the distance and then smiled and said, "It was beautiful!" For my Dad, it was a memorable experience of wonder.

During a visit to see my Dad some years after my Mom died, we were walking out together to my car as I was preparing to leave that evening. It was a beautiful, clear, starlit night. He was in his mid-eighties at this point. He looked up to the sky and commented with all the awe and wonder of a little schoolboy. As I recall, I looked up to the sky a little jaded and thought, *Oh well, it's the stars again.*

That night I envied my Dad. After all those years, he had not lost his sense of wonder.

> *"Wonder is something we see or perceive that causes our spirits to soar and our minds to marvel at a world we discover beyond our own."*
>
> Janet Chester Bly

David seems to experience a similar wonder. "When I consider Your heavens, the work of Your fingers, the moon and the stars, which You have ordained; What is man that You take thought of him, and he son of man that You care for him?" (Psalm 8:3–4 NASB).

In my experience, getting wounded in this world can literally knock the wonder right out of you.

But, to live in a world full of wonders (if you have the capacity to see them) without a loving and powerful God that you can have a relationship with seems very dull and boring to me.

The grace of God is continuing to enable me to both regain and increase my own capacity to wonder. Do you still have the capacity to wonder? If not, where did it get lost?

Want more? Check out these resources:
Janet Chester Bly, *Awakening Your Sense of Wonder*.

Richard Beck, *Hunting Magic Eels*

30

SIN: CONFESSION, REPENTANCE AND HEALING

*Now, theologically, that fundamental immaturity is the effect
of sin. And it's very serious business. If you can't talk about
sin, you're like a farmer who can't talk about weeds and
bugs: The bugs get fatter and the weeds get taller. So, we
have to talk about sin, **because sin is a matter of the will's
distortion of the whole person** [emphasis added].*

Dallas Willard

I know by this point some followers of Jesus may be thinking or
saying to themselves, *Come on, guy. What about sin, the real
problem? Enough of this brokenness stuff!* There is clearly a
connection between confession of sin and healing.

> When I kept silent about my sin, my body wasted away
> through my groaning all day long. For day and night Thy
> hand was heavy upon me; my vitality was drained away
> as with the fever-heat of summer. I acknowledged my

sin to Thee, and my iniquity I did not hide; I said, "I will confess my transgression to the Lord"; and Thou didst forgive the guilt of my sin. (Psalm 32: 3–5 NASB)

"Therefore, confess your sins to one another, and pray for one another, so that you may be healed."

(James 5:16 NASB).

Sin is and always will be our biggest problem. But do the Scriptures teach that sin is the only and exclusive reason that Jesus died on the cross? The word *sin* has fallen out of favor in our vocabulary today, so here are a few definitions to help us understand what many consider a rather archaic term. Sadly, it seems that, among many, sin is becoming an increasingly irrelevant term as well.

Timothy Keller said, "Sin is not only doing bad things, but it is also when good things become ultimate things."

For many people, finding a spouse is a good thing, but it's not an ultimate thing. Seamands illustrates Keller's point, "If they work at it, men make good husbands and women make good wives. But they make lousy gods."[112]

Deep disappointment always follows anytime we attempt to make a good thing into the ultimate thing. Imperfect human beings simply cannot bear the full weight of being someone else's world, entire purpose for living, or their everything. We were never designed to carry such a crushing load. Neither was fame or fortune, although some things seem to create the illusion of the ultimate better than others.

Whenever you seek the ultimate in the temporal, you will be disappointed and disillusioned in the end. Only a power greater than ourselves can bear the full weight of our existence. John Ortberg stated, "The soul integrates the will and mind and body. Sin disintegrates them."[113]

The original Greek word for sin, *hamartia*, was an archer's term that literally meant "missing the mark." It means missing how God intends us to live, disregarding His design, and loving limits for our life. Bill Bright, president and founder of what is now called Cru, said that sin could be defined as "active rebellion or passive indifference" toward God.

Thomas Merton said, "All sin starts from the assumption that my false self, the self that exists only in my own egocentric desires, is the fundamental reality of life to which everything else in the universe is ordered."

Sin is a huge problem. It is the primary reason Jesus died on the cross. But sin was never intended to win the day. "Then the Lord said to Cain, 'Why are you angry? And why has your countenance fallen? If you do well, will not your countenance be lifted up? And if you do not do well, sin is crouching at the door; and its desire is for you, but you must master it'" (Genesis 4:6–7 NASB).

Unfortunately, the Bible records that Cain lost his battle with sin, and so have any others in this struggle since that day. But a new hope arose when God sent His own Son, Jesus, into the world. His birth, life, death, burial, resurrection, and ascension have provided us this opportunity:

> Therefore do not let sin reign in your mortal body that you should obey its lusts, and do not go on presenting the members of your body as instruments of unrighteousness, but present yourselves to God as those

alive from the dead, and your members as instruments of righteousness to God. For sin shall not be master over you, for you are not under law, but under grace. (Romans 6:12–14 NASB).

In summary, sin is to be confessed, repented of, and forsaken through God's grace and power. As a general rule, brokenness is to be acknowledged and substantially healed through God's grace and power.

GRACE ENCOUNTER: GRATITUDE

There are days and times while writing this book and through the course of my life that I have experienced an enormous amount of gratitude. The positive psychology movement has led to a resurgence of interest in the many health benefits of gratitude in our popular culture. There is nothing new about the power of gratitude.

One of the winter holiday season movies I enjoy seeing each year is *White Christmas.* One of my favorite songs is the duet between Bing Crosby and Rosemary Clooney, "Counting My Blessings." As only Bing could sing it, "When I'm worried and cannot sleep, I count my blessings instead of sheep, and I go to sleep counting my blessings."

I also grew up singing the old hymn at FBC, Owenton, "Count Your Blessings." The refrain goes,

> Count your blessings, name them one by one,
>> Count your blessings, see what God has done.
>>> Count your blessings.
>>> Name … them … one … by … one.
>> Count your many blessings see what God has done.

31
CHAPTER

INTEGRATIVE MEDICINE

"Integrative medicine is applying diet, supplementing diet when needed, exercise and healthy lifestyle with conventional medicine for patient's best outcome" (Kentuckiana Integrative Medicine Association [KIIMA] website).

I believe in many ways that I grew up in the golden age of medicine. Cures were discovered for major diseases like polio and tuberculosis. I grew up in a small community where what our two local doctors said about your health was considered gospel.

I am no longer quite as trusting in conventional medicine as I once was. Don't get me wrong. I still believe in the medical model of healing up to a point. There are still a lot of good health-care professionals out there. When I get sick, I still go to see my primary care physician. Since colon cancer runs in my family, I still go for regular screenings for this and will continue to do so in the future.

In my mid-fifties, I began to struggle with physical exhaustion. I thought one possible source of my exhaustion could be something wrong with my thyroid. Over a two-year period, I had blood work done at my primary care physician's office and was told repeatedly,

"The lab work on your thyroid looks fine." I trusted them that I did not have a thyroid problem, but I still was given no other reasons why I was battling with physical exhaustion.

A professional colleague of mine whom I work with at North Springs had been telling me about an integrative medicine doctor she had been seeing for years that had helped her immensely. My frustration with feeling exhausted most of the time finally pushed me to seek a second opinion. I chose to see my colleague's integrative medicine doctor. I am forever grateful that I did.

I had to complete a detailed written medical history prior to my first appointment. Dr. Alan McDaniel spent one and a half hours with me during my initial appointment, which was by far the most extensive and thorough medical history I have ever received. He then sent me to have some rather extensive lab work completed. Instead of running only one test on my thyroid, TSH, he requested six different tests on my thyroid.

He uttered the results, "You have Hashimoto's disease, an autoimmune disorder of the thyroid, which is definitely treatable."

My lab work also indicated that I had a condition known in the integrative medicine world as adrenal exhaustion. Many, if not most, in the conventional medicine world do not even believe this condition exists. To treat these conditions and other low levels (some low mineral levels discovered through hair analysis), it was recommended I take high quality nutritional supplements. In some cases, I was offered a choice between medication or supplements.

My improvement was not dramatic or overnight, but I slowly began to feel better. At this season of my life, I no longer battle with daily physical exhaustion. In many ways, most days, I feel better than I have in years.

32
CHAPTER

BRAIN HEALTH PERSPECTIVE

Example of Addressing Both Physical and Mental Dimensions

I don't remember when I was first introduced to the work of psychiatrist Daniel Amen, MD, but I've been fascinated by the findings of the thousands of SPECT scans he has completed on his patients. Dr. Amen has the distinction of examining more SPECT scans than anyone living. SPECT, or Single Photon Emission Computed Tomography, is a nuclear medicine approach where a radioactive isotope is injected in your bloodstream, and then you are put under a scan that highlights activity in different regions of the brain. From this, you can see certain regions of the brain that are "too hot," meaning too active or regions with very low activity. According to Dr. Amen, areas of the brain that are too active need to be calmed down, and areas of the brain where the activity is too low need to be stimulated.

At the end of 2013, I decided to order Dr. Amen's *Brain and Behavior* DVD series and make it available to our staff at North Springs for enrichment and continuing education. This included a large binder of materials and some of the questionnaires used at the Amen Clinics. The two questionnaires that were used at that time by the clinical historian at his centers were the Amen General Symptom Checklist and the Amen Brain System Checklist (updated and available online now as the Brain Health Assessment).

At considerable personal and professional risk (just kidding), I completed the two questionnaires and asked my wife to complete the questionnaires on me as someone who knows me well. She gave me one of those concerned looks. "This is not going to come back on me negatively, is it?" I gave my best effort to convince her it would not, and both she and I completed the questionnaires on my behalf.

As I tallied up and scored the results, I can't say I was surprised to find out that the area of my brain that was the "hottest" or most overactive was the anterior cingulate region. Through what I was learning from the *Brain and Behavior* DVD series, along with Dr. Amen's writings, I began to treat the overactivity in this region of my brain with a minimum of 1,000 milligrams (EPA + DHA) of high-quality fish oil. I also began a trial of 5-HTP, beginning with 50 milligrams in the midafternoon, and a week or two later, I added 50 milligrams at bedtime.

About this same time, through reading another book, I discovered the writings of Julia Ross, MA, and her book, *The Mood Cure*, which in many ways supported what I was learning from Dr. Amen. The effect of taking these two supplements was gradual, but I could absolutely tell after a few weeks that my brain was beginning to function better.

Dr. Amen has been quoted in saying, "Even mild traumatic brain injury (TBI) can significantly alter the quality of someone's life." Is it possible that there are literally hundreds of thousands of people that could be walking around with mild to moderate brain injury, who may be functioning in life at a reasonably high level, but far from optimally? Even though I had not been diagnosed with a mild TBI at this time, I later learned that this was clearly part of my story.

Several of our clinical staff and myself streamed a three-day Amen Clinic conference in late January 2017. As a conference participant, I had the opportunity to receive a SPECT scan at a significantly reduced fee, and I had to decide in one week whether to take advantage of this discount. I had been thinking about getting a scan for at least five years. I thought I may never get a deal like this again and called the Amen Clinic in Atlanta to set up an appointment.

No medical professional was suggesting that I take this course of action. Two weeks before my appointment, my wife asked me, "Now tell me again why you want to go to Atlanta and have your brain scanned?"

I replied, "Dr. Amen says you are your best self when your brain is working at its best. I've been wondering for some time with my history of taking strong medication for years for a seizure disorder, enduring three long-term exposures to mold, and playing football for years if some brain damage may have occurred. If so, I want the chance to take steps to possibly experience some healing in these areas. For the rest of the years I have remaining, I want to be the best husband, best parent, best grandparent, and best counselor and life coach."

She just looked at me with a slight smile and replied, "Okay."

I made the pilgrimage to the Amen Clinic in Atlanta and had the two separate SPECT scans (resting and concentration) completed over a two-day period.

My doctor met with me to begin to interpret the results of my brain scans. A lot of the mystery of what I had suspected for years was now over. I had been functioning for years with an old mild TBI, diagnosed when I had the SPECT scan at the Amen Clinic in Atlanta in March 2017.

The doctor stated, "You really took a big lick to the back of your head at some point when you were younger. Do you remember when this happened?"

I had to confess that I was not sure. This was an eye-opening and absolutely incredible experience for me. It's been said, "A picture is worth a thousand words." This was never truer for me when I was actually able to see pictures of my brain!

The doctor who interpreted my scans (resting and concentration) drew a circle with a white marker around the entire cingulate (anterior, middle, and posterior) region of my brain. He commented, "This would have been much worse if you had not been already treating it over the past few years."

The treatment recommendations in this area for me would continue to be a combination of high-quality pharmaceutical grade fish oil to address the mild TBI I had experienced in my past. He recommended that I increase the level of fish oil that I was already taking to promote further healing for the mild TBI.

To address the anterior cingulate gyrus region that was still too active, he recommended I increase the levels of 5-HTP (a precursor to the development of serotonin) in a moderate amount for more optimal benefit. He also encouraged me to start using a pharmaceutical grade form of 5-HTP as well.

Dr. Amen describes the basal ganglia region as "the anxiety thermostat" of the brain. I had been tolerating and functioning with a low level of anxiety for years, and I would always just tell myself, "This is just me."

My scan revealed that the basal ganglia region of my brain was overactive, and you could see where it worsened on the concentration scan. He recommended for me a nutraceutical[114] that was a blend of several natural ingredients at levels clinically proven to help reduce stress, restore calm, and manage occasional anxiety without causing sleepiness.

A SPECT scan gives you much more clear information as to where to target interventions in your brain to hopefully encourage more balanced functioning in these areas. As I followed my treatment recommendations by taking the recommended nutraceuticals, I am now totally convinced that my brain is functioning more optimally.

On the trip home from Atlanta, I shed a few tears and had some compassion for my old brain that has been struggling for so many years. I now wonder whether I would have been able to complete the book you are now reading had I not received the SPECT scans and followed the recommendations. I am daily grateful that I am now able to experience what Dr. Amen likes to say, "You are your best self when your brain is working at its best."

Want more? Check out these resources:
Amen Clinics, www.amenclinics.com

Brain MD, www.brainMD.com

Brain Health Assessment, www.brainhealthassessment.com

33
CHAPTER

THE IMPORTANCE OF ATTENTION

attention

- the act or state of applying the mind to something
- a condition of readiness for such attention involving especially a selective narrowing or focusing of consciousness and receptivity
- consideration with a view to action an act of civility or courtesy, especially in courtship
- sympathetic consideration of the needs and wants of others[115]

"Whenever we act on our world, whether intentionally or automatically, we employ the function of the mind called attention. Attention can be considered the ignition key of the mind. A vast array of our mental and physical actions follow what we attend to" (Curt Thompson, *The Anatomy of the Soul*, 51).

Are we slowly losing our ability to give sustained focused attention to anything in our fast-paced information age? Before going to the Amen Clinic in Atlanta to have a SPECT scan (resting and concentration), if you had asked me whether I thought I might have a form of ADD, I would have answered rather confidently, "Absolutely not!" So, what a surprise it was for me to receive the news when I had the scans read and compared in the afternoon on the second day that I *did* have a form of ADD.

In the previous section, Brain Health PerSPECTive, I had to follow the treatment recommendations for the other areas of my brain for two weeks before beginning to address the ADD symptoms. This would involve addressing a decrease in functioning I was experiencing in the prefrontal cortex (PFC) area. Dr. Amen has learned in his years of research that you have stabilized some regions of the brain first (temporal lobes and basal ganglia) before attempting to intervene in other areas. The overactivity in my basal ganglia region had to be treated first before attempting to stimulate the PFC area. If not, adding a stimulant too soon to help the PFC would likely worsen the overactivity in the basal ganglia region, thereby increasing anxiety.

I received the resting SPECT scan on day one and the concentration scan on day two. When the two scans were compared on day two, you could clearly see areas of my PFC that had worsened when I was trying to concentrate! This was somewhat shocking to me because as I mentioned earlier, I never would have imagined that I had a form of ADD.

Two weeks after I had begun the other treatments, I was able to add a nutraceutical form of the nutrient Tyrosine (l-tyrosine), a precursor of the neurotransmitter's dopamine and norepinephrine.[116] I was encouraged to take this thirty minutes before a meal for more optimal absorption because it does not compete well with other nutrients. My ability to focus and concentrate has absolutely been enhanced through the addition of this nutraceutical.

As mentioned earlier, this is clearly an intervention in the stature/ physical dimension of healing. For me, this has substantially enhanced further the "favor with God and men"/spiritual and social dimensions of my life.

Please note that a nutraceutical approach to addressing some mental or emotional challenge that you may be facing will absolutely be dependent on your unique, individual responses to some of Dr. Amen's checklists and/or your own personal SPECT scan results. There is also a medical disclaimer on these assessments.

Want more? Check out this resource.

ADD Type Test, www.addtypetest.com

34

CHAPTER

FIVE WAYS THAT JESUS HEALED BLINDNESS

What can we learn from the Great Physician? John Eldredge introduced me to this incredible idea.[117] Remember, this is just the five ways Jesus healed blindness that are recorded. John reminds us in his gospel account, "Jesus did many other things as well. If every one of them were written down, I suppose that even the whole world would not have room for the books that would be written."[118]

In Mark 8:22–25 (NIV), it reads,

> They came to Bethsaida, and some people brought a blind man and begged Jesus to touch him. He took the blind man by the hand and led him outside the village. When he had spit on the man's eyes and put his hands on him, Jesus asked, "Do you see anything?"
>
> He looked up and said, "I see people; they look like trees walking around."

Once more Jesus put his hands on the man's eyes. Then his eyes were opened, his sight was restored, and he saw everything clearly.

Specific Methods/Approach

He took his hand, walked outside of the village, spit on the man's eyes (obviously not an insult when Jesus did this in the context of healing back in the day), put His hands on him, and asked him a clarifying question.

I absolutely marvel at this passage. It is Jesus applying His healing methods, and at first, the man's blindness is only partially cured. Jesus again put His hands on the man's eyes, and he was completely cured.

So, what does this say about we mere humans in the healing arts when our attempts and methods to help someone do not immediately bring healing or restoration? Jesus's example here is so encouraging to me. Obviously, some approaches will require more specific probing clarifying questions, patience, and gentle persistence.

This idea of gentle persistence can be encouraging for many, including both the practitioners in the healing professions and the clients and patients they are attempting to serve.

Two Blind Men Receive Sight (Matthew 20:29–34 NIV)

As Jesus and his disciples were leaving Jericho, a large crowd followed him. [30] Two blind men were sitting by the roadside, and when they heard that Jesus was going by, they shouted, "Lord, Son of David, have mercy on us!"

The crowd rebuked them and told them to be quiet, but they shouted all the louder, "Lord, Son of David, have mercy on us!"

Jesus stopped and called them. "What do you want me to do for you?" he asked.

"Lord," they answered, "we want our sight."

Jesus had compassion on them and touched their eyes. Immediately they received their sight and followed Him.

Specific Methods/Approach

He asked a specific question about what they wanted. It is incredible to me that Jesus would ask what they wanted (as the God-man, didn't he already know?), even though it may have seemed obvious to many. Remember how I said earlier that God wants to invite us into a dialogue? Notice that healing occurred after the invitation to dialogue. Also notice how this is a focused intervention on just the two of them. He felt compassion for them and touched their eyes. Their sight was restored completely. They became followers.

Luke 18:35–43 (NIV) (Similar Account in Mark 10:46–52)

As Jesus approached Jericho, a blind man was sitting by the roadside begging. When he heard the crowd going by, he asked what was happening. They told him, "Jesus of Nazareth is passing by."

He called out, "Jesus, Son of David, have mercy on me!"

Those who led the way rebuked him and told him to be quiet, but he shouted all the more, "Son of David, have mercy on me!"

Jesus stopped and ordered the man to be brought to him. When he came near, Jesus asked him, "What do you want me to do for you?"

"Lord, I want to see," he replied.

Jesus said to him, "Receive your sight; your faith has healed you." Immediately he received his sight and followed Jesus, praising God. When all the people saw it, they also praised God.

Specific Methods/Approach

He asked a specific question and spoke the command, "Receive your sight." Notice how Jesus mentioned his faith was instrumental in his healing, but faith was not mentioned as a factor in the previous passage. He became a follower. My question again: what if, for some, the experience of substantial healing is a significant influence in their decision to be a follower of Jesus?

John 9:1–7 (NIV)

As he went along, he saw a man blind from birth. His disciples asked him, "Rabbi, who sinned, this man or his parents, that he was born blind?"

"Neither this man nor his parents sinned," said Jesus, "but this happened so that the works of God might be displayed in him. As long as it is day, we must do the works of him who sent me. Night is coming, when no one can work. While I am in the world, I am the light of the world."

After saying this, he spit on the ground, made some mud with the saliva, and put it on the man's eyes. "Go," he told him, "wash in the Pool of Siloam" (this word means "sent"). So, the man went and washed, and came home seeing.

Specific Methods/Approach

He responded to a specific religious question posed about a man blind from birth. Please notice the gravity of Jesus saying that "neither this man nor his parents sinned," so this man's condition of blindness had nothing to do with sin. By saying this and healing the man, Jesus also challenged one of the prevailing religious beliefs of his day, that sin was the cause of all suffering. He then spit on the ground, made some mud with the saliva, put it on the man's eyes, and told him to wash it off in a specific body of water. He was cured of blindness (restoration of his sight, made more whole).

Let's be clear in this passage that (v. 3), "so that the works of God might be displayed in him," clearly involves healing and restoration. While some are healed and others are not will forever remain a mystery to me this side of heaven.

So, what if we earnestly seek healing and are not substantially healed? The apostle Paul's experience is illustrative here. He wrote about "a thorn in my flesh." There is some mystery about what this was, so the specifics of his struggle we are not sure. Paul continues, "Three times I pleaded with the Lord to take it away from me. But he said to me, 'My grace is sufficient for you, for my power is made perfect in weakness.' Therefore, I will boast all the more gladly about my weaknesses, so that Christ's power may rest on me."[119]

Matthew 12:22 (NIV)

Then they brought him a demon-possessed man who was blind and mute, and Jesus healed him so that he could both talk and see.

Specific Methods/Approach

Here it seems the person whom Jesus healed appears to be unable to act in his own best interest, so others brought him to Jesus. This has some of the elements of a classic intervention today. I believe he still had to be cooperative enough to be brought. Jesus healed him so he could both see and speak. No specific methods or approaches used are given.

1. Jesus employed several different methods/approaches in the healing of blindness. By this example, shouldn't we be a little bit leery of one-size-fits-all approaches to healing our brokenness? What if the true God who created the vast universe wanted to heal someone of their brokenness in a manner we have never seen before?

2. As a professional counselor, I and others like me have been trained in several different approaches to healing our brokenness. I also believe that there are and will be newer God-honoring methods and approaches of healing our wounds in the future.

3. While many times there remains an element of mystery around healing and restoration, I believe Jesus has revealed Himself as the ultimate healer of our broken selves.

4. Through incarnational reality, the presence of Jesus can be brought to bear in our pain and suffering today.

GRACE ENCOUNTER:
FALL FRIDAY NIGHT EMBRACE

Hold on. This is not what some of you might be thinking. I was in high school playing football. Initially, I did not remember when this first occurred. Then I discovered in my scrapbook a picture of Coach Cochran greeting me while coming off the football field at the beginning of my freshman year. During the fall of my high school years, it could easily be said that I spent more quality time with my football coaches than I did with my own Dad.

Like many who played on a football team at a smaller school, I played the following teams: offense, defense, kickoff, and receiving, and I also shared punting duties and returned punts. It was usually late in the game, and we would typically be either way ahead or way behind. Coach Cochran would take me out of the game, greet me on the sidelines with a big bear hug, and say, "Good game, Hoss."

It's hard to put into words even now what this meant to me. I've mentioned earlier how I began to close myself off with the perceived safe self I was creating, to prevent getting emotionally wounded deeply again. Part of the unintended result of this was feeling more isolated and lonelier. The acceptance and approval I felt in those Friday night embraces from my coach was life giving to this internally isolated adolescent.

I've come to learn that men need the strong and pure embrace of other men. I don't know if my Dad got many hugs from his Dad (my grandfather), but I don't ever remember my Dad giving me a hug. I recall being hugged very infrequently during my childhood and adolescence at home. I remember telling people I met in college, "I did not grow up in a 'huggy' family."

The hug and strong verbal affirmation from Coach Cochran, whom I both feared and respected (those who knew him will know what I mean), meant the world to me back then. Coach Cochran could be a tough customer to deal with, but deep down, I always knew he genuinely cared for me. To this day, I still cherish those moments.

Why all the athletic stories? I now believe that success in athletics was a grace gift that provided me a level of affirmation I was not receiving fully in other areas of my life. I can now see how athletics (and academics as well) provided me this affirmation through a season of my life until I understood and began to experience that my heavenly Father had desired to more fully affirm me all along. This divine affirmation has been experienced in greater depth as I have been and am being more substantially healed from my own brokenness.

Men and women of all ages benefit from appropriate, nonsexual touch, to be embraced and affirmed by those who care for them deeply. It is also both healing and affirming and even promotes overall health and well-being. Children, adolescents, and young adults who are deprived of meaningful and appropriate touch are much more vulnerable to unsavory characters who may want to use them and take advantage of them.

To be careful here, I am not advocating walking up to and indiscriminately hugging complete strangers. Even if it is someone you know, if you are uncertain how they might respond if you were to hug them, ask permission. "May I give you a hug?" If it is someone you don't know well or a person you do know with poor boundaries, putting your hand out for a handshake is still an appropriate touch.

35

LIVING WITH BROKEN DREAMS

I had dreamed of playing college athletics since I was very young, and the place where I wanted to play was the University of Kentucky. Both of my parents and my older brother Larry had graduated from there. My great uncle, Al Muth, lettered in football at UK in 1919. He also played baseball at UK. In the *Kentuckian* (1922) college yearbook, it stated:

> Albert Muth, outfielder. "Al," one of the best outfielders who ever wore the Blue and White, has played four years with the Wildcats and made a record any player would be proud to claim. For consistency in the field there was not a man on the team that can compare with him.

A serious knee injury in my senior year of high school sidelined me for most of the football season. About midseason, a northern Kentucky paper interviewed our head football coach, Roy Cochran. We were still undefeated at midseason (6-0), despite having several players injured. Coach Cochran mentioned me getting injured in the article and stated, "Kentucky had already had a couple of looks at him." The news of that interest continued to fuel my desire to pursue playing football at UK.

I decided to walk on the football team at UK in the fall of 1976. My introduction to college football was "safe and slow" for the first week and a half of preseason practice. I believe I might have been one of the first players to try to join the team with a diagnosed seizure disorder. I jogged around the practice field for a week and a half until I was finally medically released to fully participate in practice.

While I played both tight end and wide receiver in high school, I walked on as a wide receiver. Some interesting things began to happen at the tight end position. Two freshman tight ends on scholarship left the team before the season started. Then another walk-on tight end left the team as well.

Shortly after these events occurred, one day in practice, one of the scout team coaches yelled out, "Need a tight end!"

I was standing in a long line of wide receivers, and without hesitating, I ran over to the tight end spot. I remained the tight end on the scout team offense for the entire season. This was by far my biggest contribution to the eventual success of this team.

As a result of being on the scout team offense, I saw a considerable amount of playing time in all four junior varsity games that year. (We were 2-2.) However, as a freshman, I was still too far down the depth chart to suit up or see any varsity action during the regular season. This Kentucky Wildcat football team finished the regular season at 9-2 and then received and accepted an invitation to the Peach Bowl.

I had the privilege and opportunity to travel with the team and dress out for the Peach Bowl. As a little added extra, it was fun to "get a little ink" and be interviewed by *The Cats Pause* prior to the Peach Bowl. We played North Carolina and wound up winning the game and shutting them out, 21-0. The lead up to the game, warming up, being on the sidelines, and celebrating the win were all very memorable and enjoyable experiences I will always treasure.

I returned to UK for the spring semester and participated in winter workouts with the team. That winter, I added at least fifteen pounds of muscle to my frame and was the strongest physically I've ever been. Early that spring, we all went down to the UK track and were timed in the forty-yard dash. I ran the forty in 4.6 seconds, so as I gained size and strength, I think I got a little bit faster as well.

We were told at the beginning of winter workouts that two scholarships were going to be awarded to two walk-ons. I worked as hard as I could to be in a position to receive one of those scholarships. I was now hoping that this was going to be my big chance.

On day one or two after suiting up and starting spring practice, I was participating in a drill. I attempted to cut hard on my left knee (the knee I had surgery on in high school) to avoid a tackler, and the knee completely gave out. I was tackled, and the following few moments as I slowly got up off the field felt like an eternity to me. It was as if my entire athletic life flashed before me, and the painful realization began to dawn on me that my football days were over.

I was unable to finish spring practice. My hope of earning a scholarship vanished, and a big part of my identity as a student-athlete was lost. The technology was simply not available to fully repair knee injuries like mine as it is today. In an ironic twist, almost thirty years later, I was finally accurately diagnosed with an ACL tear and underwent reconstructive surgery with a donor ligament.

It could easily be said that as a part of my body was broken during this injury in spring practice, a big part of my spirit was broken as well. The hymn writer's cry, "come and heal my broken spirit," was applicable at this time in my own story. The challenge for me was, in my spiritual journey up to that point, I was truly unaware and was never taught or encouraged in any of my religious upbringing, that I could pray and avail myself of other resources for the healing of my broken spirit.

Time had passed, but I still was not completely ready to give up on some of my dreams of continuing to compete as an athlete at the collegiate level. I decided to walk on the track team at UK the second semester of my sophomore year. I trained hard that winter with the team, and that spring was given the opportunity to compete in a meet at Eastern Kentucky University with the track teams from the University of Louisville and Cumberland College as well. Even though I ran a personal best in the 440-yard dash (now the 400 meters) and finished third, I was quite disappointed with my time. This was the only meet in college that my brother and I competed together at the same meet. He (Jim) was running the mile and/or two miles for Cumberland College.

There are dreams that we all have that may not come to complete fruition in this lifetime. Living with unrealized dreams can be a painful part of our journey here. For several years, I "shouted at the heavens" for an explanation of why. The answer to the age-old question, "If God were good and loving, then why did He allow _____ to happen?" Here are just a few of my own questions:

- Why did my Mom die when she did?
- Why did my older brother (from my Dad's first marriage) die so young?
- Why did a committed relationship I was in not go the distance?

With all these questions, I finally quit demanding answers and began to embrace the mystery that is so much a part of this life. It is also strangely comforting that the same God who I have been mad at for not answering all my questions is the God who has promised He will never leave me alone in the midst of my struggle.

My story and yours has not completely been written. No matter what happens in the balance of this life, I hold fast to the belief that ultimately my future will be good. Dan Allender writes, "Wisdom ultimately isn't a formula or a conclusion but a way of being in the world that leads to a more truthful and more beautiful good."

GRACE ENCOUNTER: "SPEAK WORDS": A TIMELY CONVERSATION

Leanne Payne said, "It is in dialogue with others that we come to know ourselves."

I graduated from UK with a bachelor's degree in business administration in May 1981. I began to question how well I could live out my faith in the corporate business world, especially after I took a class at UK called "The Legal Environment of Business," where I learned terms like "strategic misrepresentation," which my instructor said was being taught at the Harvard School of Business. It was essentially lying about your own company in an attempt to win a contract or lying in order to gain a marketing advantage over a competitor. I became somewhat disillusioned about going into business, but also experienced just a general unrest whether this was going to be a good vocational fit for me.

After graduation from UK, I really had no clear sense of what to do next. I'd been serving part time as a youth leader in my home church in Owenton, doing some odd jobs that included substitute teaching and being an assistant middle school football coach while attempting to sort out the next step in my life.

My brother Jim had gone to Cumberland College on a track and cross-country scholarship. He had come to faith in Christ as a student at Cumberland College and was, what we would say the country, "on fire for God." He was now in his senior year and came home for a few days during the Christmas holidays of 1981.

Late one evening, we sat down together at our parents' kitchen table, and he proceeded to present the following opportunity to me. His pitch to me went something like this:

> Mom and Dad had said you have expressed some interest in getting your teacher certification. Why don't you come back to Cumberland College with me and work on it? We can room together. You can take some Bible classes there and attend the same church I do. And who knows? You might meet a nice Christian girl there.

I took my brother up on this offer, packed up my bags, and was admitted into Cumberland College for the January 1982 spring semester. This was a totally life-altering conversation for me, and I am forever grateful to my brother for having the courage to pitch this opportunity to me. Key decisions were made while at Cumberland College that fundamentally altered and set the course for the rest of my life. This was a major grace encounter.

Are there some wise, caring individuals that you permit to speak into your life? No man (or woman) is an island. I believe one of the primary purposes of the church is to be a rich source of authentic community, which has the potential to be absolutely healing in many ways.

36
CHAPTER

HEALING FROM REJECTION

It's been said that rejection is a gut-wrenching experience, and I can personally attest to this. While stress can manifest itself in our bodies in different ways, it has typically gone to my gut. I am quite confident that I inherited this tendency from my mom. In high school, if you could not find me an hour before the game, some of my teammates would likely say, "You can probably find him in the bathroom." (Sorry for some of you who are thinking, *TMI*.) While I dated some in high school, I never dated anyone steady and really never had a steady girlfriend through high school.

I can remember being in a little embarrassed when my Mom was hosting the Homemakers Club in our home and commented to one of the women in attendance, "I'm a little worried about Joe. He's not dated that much, and I'm afraid he's going to fall in love with the first girl he meets when he goes to college."

Mom was right. It happened. I fell in love in college. I also remember the aftermath of being rejected by this romantic interest. I was in gut-wrenching pain for several days following this. I even went to student health services, thinking I might have a lower GI viral infection because of my frequent trips to the bathroom. I can still remember the medical professional that saw me that day asking, "Have you been under some considerable stress lately?"

Throughout the course of my life, I have collected my share of rejection experiences. Even though these were painful experiences, there was a tendency to minimize the impact of these experiences, especially as a man, where we may have been culturally conditioned to minimize all kinds of pain and distress.

In 2011, I was listening to a CD of a Pastoral Care Ministries event that occurred in 2007. The presenter, Mark Pertuit, mentioned three ways we get wounded/broken:

1. Some form of deprivation or neglect—begins with parents or parent figures. A parent's emotional absence is an example.
2. Rejection—by parents, peers, etc. "Someone told you, 'You're not good.'"
3. Abuse—misuse of power, e.g., sexual abuse through looks, words, or touch.[120]

For the first time, something I tried to minimize and tell myself, "It's not a big deal" was being seriously considered as a really big deal, right along beside abuse and neglect. When I had some time to myself, I said a prayer, took out a pad of paper, and began to list all the rejection experiences I could remember, including those where I remember rejecting someone else. I was a little surprised that I filled up several pages of rejection experiences.

I can still remember the Friday evening when my wife was out of town and I was home by myself, with the exception of our dog, Jackson. I began to pray over the rejection experiences one by one, asking God to forgive me when I had rejected someone else, and I forgave those who had rejected me and asked God to heal my heart.

I am totally convinced God honored this time of prayer as I felt lighter the next day and I had experienced some significant healing as a result.

GRACE ENCOUNTER: HEALTHY, MUTUALLY RESPECTFUL RELATIONSHIPS

This, for the professional counselor/therapist, would be referred to as "the therapeutic relationship." Some of my colleagues in the field believe that it is not the counseling theory or technique that is the most important part of the healing process, but the therapeutic relationship is the most important healing dimension.

As we all should know, this is not limited by any means to the counseling office. Appropriate healthy relationships that are mutually respectful and mutually reciprocal, that have a high level of trust and good boundaries, can be quite healing.

37
CHAPTER

BENEFICIAL SOLITUDE

Blaise Pascal said, "I have discovered that all the unhappiness of men arises from one single fact, that they are unable to stay quietly in their own room." When you're wired as an introvert as I am, you look forward to and pursue opportunities for solitude. My wife gave me one of those *Don't Sweat the Small Stuff* books a few years ago. This one was on marriage. I read on the back cover some of what the wife and co-author enjoyed doing with their free time. She listed the following: horseback riding, time with family and friends, **solitude**. I thought to myself, *Wow, she actually said this out loud (or in print)*. In my struggle with feeling overly responsible, I've wrestled with guilt at times when I sensed a longing to spend time alone. I would have the thought, *Isn't this really just being selfish?*

I've learned for myself that this is really an integral part of my own self-care. Don't get me wrong. I enjoy spending time with friends and family. But for me to be at my best, I have to balance time with people with time alone. For the introvert, solitude is absolutely restorative. After I've spent time alone, I'm a better friend, counselor, father, and husband. You get the picture.

I've travelled alone to some different retreat centers in relatively close proximity to where I live. It's totally quiet in my room with the exception of the gentle hum of my laptop computer. I feel strangely content and then counter my own thought, *What is strange about it?*

I hold in my hands a copy of the book, *Introvert Power*, by Laurie Helgoe, PhD, and on the back cover near the bottom are the following phrases: "QUIET IS MIGHT. SOLITUDE IS STRENGTH. INTROVERSION IS POWER."

As I typed these phrases, the song came to me, "And I say to myself, what a wonderful world." And I smiled.

"At daybreak Jesus went out to a solitary place" (Luke 4:42 NIV).

GRACE ENCOUNTER: NEVER ALONE

I was in late elementary school or early middle school. On Sunday mornings at FBC, Owenton, all children in this age range would first meet in a larger assembly before breaking off into smaller Bible study classes. Here, announcements would be made, and we would sing a few hymns (songs) together. It was "request time" with Marvin Ray Stewart, our pianist, a bigger-than-life personality with a booming voice and a big laugh.

He would ask for requests of hymns to sing, and without fail, my friends and I would yell out in unison, "Four hundred!" When we turned together in the old Baptist hymnal, hymn number four hundred was "Never Alone." We would sing this hymn with great gusto, especially in the chorus, when the boys who were my friends and I would sing (really almost yell out), "No, never alone, No, never alone, He promised never to leave me, never to leave me alone." We really punched the word *no* each time. I think that maybe little boys saying *no* really loud in church just felt good at the time.

What an absolutely profound truth for the Christ follower. Nick Cruz, a gang member converted to Christ, wrote a book a number of years ago with the title, *Lonely, But Never Alone*. Loneliness is one of those examples of unavoidable pain we all experience at times living in a less-than-perfect world. But even in the times of loneliness I've experienced, there is this mystical and inescapable sense that I'm not completely alone. In a way that I will never be able to completely explain or fully understand, the Holy Spirit, third person of the Trinity, took up residence in my life the moment I opened my heart up and invited Christ in.

Since that moment, the existential aloneness that some people experience, sensing they are "all alone in the universe," this depth of loneliness has been a rare experience for me.

HEALING THROUGH ENCOURAGEMENT

"Bind Up"

שָׁבַח (ḥā·ḇǎš): v.

Encourage, formally, bind up, that is, **speak words which hearten and enliven** one's feelings and attitudes, as a figurative extension of bandaging up a wound (Isaiah 61:1+)

"Reckless words pierce like a sword, **but the tongue of the wise brings healing** *[emphasis added]"*

(Proverbs 12:18 NIV).

Remember some of the profound ways we are broken in the original language definition of brokenhearted? One of the areas mentioned was courage.

The life of David illustrates at least two of the many ways we can receive encouragement. Jonathan encouraged David. "And Jonathan, Saul's son, arose and went to David at Horesh, and encouraged him in God" (1 Samuel 23:16 NASB).

David "encouraged himself in the Lord." "And David was greatly distressed; for the people spoke of stoning him, because the soul of all the people was grieved, every man for his sons and for his daughters: but David encouraged himself in the LORD his God" (1 Samuel 30:6 AKJV).

Speak words which hearten and enliven one's feelings and attitudes.

39

CHAPTER

COUNSELING ...
FOR ME? HOW ABOUT YOU?

The purposes of a man's heart are deep waters, but a man of
understanding draws them out.

Proverbs 20:5, NIV

Even in crystal clear water, when it gets deep enough, we can only see so far down. This is why we all desperately need "people of understanding" in our lives to help sort things out when the way seems unclear, confusing, and bewildering or when it temporarily seems that we have lost our way. There is a profound need for mature "people of understanding" in every family and organization, especially in the body of Christ.

Have you ever permitted or allowed a man or woman of understanding to explore some of these deep waters within you? Could counseling, life coaching, or mentoring with a wise, respected individual be an opportunity to address some potentially broken places in you and bring some healing?

My first experience of PSI in Atlanta in the fall of 1990 was an orientation. I do not remember which staff member was leading the meeting that day, but I do recall they said something like this, "If you have not been counseling before, we strongly encourage you to enter into your own counseling while you are student here at PSI."

I remember being both overconfident and unaware of my own needs that day. I looked around the classroom and said to myself, "I don't know about these other people, but I don't need counseling." As you can tell, I had quite a bit to learn.

About a year later, with my wife's persistent encouragement, I decided to enter my own counseling. We were all given a list of counseling professionals who were willing to see PSI graduate students at a reduced fee. I scanned the list and selected Jack Boyan, a PSI grad himself, who was living and working in the Atlanta area.

It turned out to be one of the best decisions I've ever made. Without going into specifics, I was encouraged, challenged, stretched, and asked probing and penetrating questions. It was also a safe place to begin to both acknowledge and examine the impact of some of the wounds I'd experienced over the years.

When I got in touch with some strong emotion, he would gently encourage me with these words, "Stay with that", which was about the last thing I wanted to do in that moment! I wanted to go around it, get over it, and avoid it, but he wanted me to feel it and journey through it. Oh, how a part of me disliked that! (But oh, how I needed it!) In many ways, I was afraid to feel.

I secretly believed for years that if I allowed myself to experience what I was feeling more deeply, I might lose control and be completely overwhelmed. No one told me—or, if they did, I wasn't listening—that I did not have to feel everything all at once, but I could pace my own journey of healing. Also, strategies can be learned to help contain strong emotion.

I continue to seek out counseling, life coaching, and mentoring opportunities. I find it especially helpful at times due to being in a leadership role. To have a confidential space to express some frustration or to help navigate some challenging and/or difficult situations or circumstances in my life. I also regularly participate in peer consultation with other respected colleagues in the field.

Men especially tend to isolate themselves, and many times they view seeking out help from someone else as a weakness. The number of military veterans and other men taking their lives through suicide should concern us all. I'll never forget taking my Dad to a medical appointment at a VA outpatient clinic late in his life and seeing a poster in the waiting room with the message:

It Takes the Courage of a Warrior to Ask for Help.

Here is my plea to all. Have the courage of a warrior and ask for help. If you can't seem to summon this courage, swallow your pride, humble yourself, and seek help anyway. No problem is beyond the reach of God for the person who wants help.

40
CHAPTER

TREATING TRAUMA AND BEYOND: EMDR

Bessel van der Kolk, trauma expert, said, "EMDR is so simple, it should've been invented thousands of years ago."[121]

I'll never forget early on in my counseling career watching a segment of a news show like *60 Minutes* or *20/20* one evening. They told the story of a twentysomething single female victim of rape who had received traditional outpatient counseling for a full year and had not gotten substantially better. She then completed six sessions of this new counseling approach called EMDR and was dramatically better. I can still remember telling myself at the end of this new segment, "I've got to learn that!"

I was able to find information on the EMDR Institute and a list of their upcoming level-one trainings in various cities across the United States. One of the upcoming trainings was going to be held in Little Rock, Arkansas. I paid for the training, booked my flight to Little Rock, completed three days of intensive level-one training, and flew back home to Kentucky.

This approach was very different than any other therapeutic modality I had ever been trained in before. Even though I felt like I was still processing a lot of information about this new approach, I was excited about the possibility of getting started with a some of my current clients. At this time in my counseling career, I was working as a mental health and chemical dependency counselor for a community mental health agency. The sites where I worked were located in some of the more rural areas around Louisville, Kentucky.

I still remember quite vividly the conversation I had with my clinical supervisor at that time, telling her what I'd learned and how I believed it could powerfully help a number of the clients that I was currently working with. She responded, "It's still a fairly new approach. I do not believe it has been researched enough yet, and you're not going to use it here."

Her reply completely took the wind out of my sails, and I basically buried all I learned about EMDR for years.

Almost fifteen years later, Northeast Christian Church in Louisville hired me as the director of their professional counseling services. Within the first month of being in this new position, one of the church's trained volunteer counselors came back from a Christian counseling conference and shared with me copies of handouts from workshops she attended at the conference. Here was one of the workshop titles: "Using Christ-Centered Visualization and EMDR in the Healing of Trauma"

I remember breathing a prayer as I was looking over this handout. "Okay, God, are You trying to get my attention here? Would You like me to pursue this approach that I've buried for all these years?"

I called the EMDR Institute again since they had updated much of the level-one resources. I was advised to complete the training again. I was informed on this call that I could repeat this updated version for half the regular price. I received this as a favorable sign and made the decision to be retrained in EMDR.

Psychologist Francine Schapiro originally discovered eye movement desensitization and reprocessing (EMDR). Dr. Shapiro experienced relief from a distressing thought on a walk by a lake after "her eyes began moving in a rapid, diagonal fashion."[122] After years of evaluating this initial experience, it was determined that her eye movements that day were a form of "bilateral stimulation" in the brain. The early EMDR trainings taught eye movements as the primary form of this bilateral stimulation (BLS). Later on, other forms of BLS, specifically tactile and audible, began to be used more frequently. I currently use the tactile form of BLS with most of my clients.

The actual reasons behind why EMDR is so effective is still not crystal clear to researchers, but what is clear is that this therapeutic modality works very effectively for many people.

As I was being trained, I recalled some of the sleep research presented in one of my classes at Georgia State University by Dr. Kenneth Matheny. I distinctly remember Dr. Matheny saying one day in class, "Rapid eye movement (REM) sleep is de-stressing."

Since I believe in a Creator God, I thought, *What a cool thing God designed, a mechanism by which our minds and bodies could de-stress while we were sleeping!*

What is believed, at least in theory, is that the experience of traumatic events somehow overwhelms our body's ability to successfully process through and discharge the distress associated with these events. I personally believe that through the use of EMDR, in a way, we are replicating the mechanism (bilateral stimulation of the brain) of REM activity in a waking state.

Since her initial discovery, Dr. Shapiro has gone on to develop her eleven-step Adaptive Information Processing (AIP) model of EMDR. I was particularly intrigued by step number seven. "The physical information processing system is like other body systems—a cut closes and heals unless blocked—physiologically geared to go toward health."[123]

This should come as no shock or surprise that a good God would create our brains and bodies to respond in this manner.

While EMDR is simple, it is not easy, and to be optimally effective, it needs to be implemented by a trained, skilled, and experienced therapist/practitioner. "It is not the bilateral stimulation that is dangerous. What is potentially dangerous is when it is not properly applied."[124]

As a professional counselor, I found EMDR to be a powerful method of healing in a variety of different contexts with clients. For clients who desire and consent to more fully integrate their faith in God in the healing process, I will use forms of invocation prayer as well in their EMDR experience.

41

BE SET FREE FAST

BSFF stands for a therapeutic modality called Be Set Free Fast, founded by psychologist Dr. Larry Nims. Dr. Nims believes that engaging the subconscious, the part of our mind that operates below our conscious level of awareness, is the key to healing in many areas of our lives. Dr. Nims states the following about our subconscious:

- continually records all our experiences
- has access to all our experiential history
- accepts all input as valid (does not make a value judgement whether it is good/bad, correct/incorrect, helpful/harmful, etc.)
- is neither a friend nor an enemy
- does whatever it has been programmed to do in each specific situation

Dr. Nims stated, "The subconscious *overrides* the conscious mind when a subconscious program is triggered and whenever a program differs from the current focus or thoughts of the conscious mind [emphasis added]."[125] This belief/finding appears to be consistent with current brain research findings reported by Dr. Caroline Leaf:

> The intrinsic activity in the nonconscious part of our minds is where most of the mind-action takes place, and it is always dominant, twenty-four hours a day. It is where we are thinking, choosing, building and sorting thoughts. Simply put, it is the constant, high-energy activity that is always going on in the nonconscious mind, even when we are resting. What we consciously think and what we say and do is all driven by the information and activity in the nonconscious mind.[126]

I had read Dr. Nims' book and become aware in an email exchange that he was a Christ follower. He emailed me his story that led to the discovery of BSFF. He reported how he had become frustrated with the limited tools he had available as a psychologist and began to pray earnestly for a better approach that could provide greater healing and hope for those he was attempting to serve. He believes that BSFF grew out of this rather lengthy time of spiritual searching.

Dr. Larry Nims, Alfred Heath, and some more of their associates offered a two-day training in BSFF in the spring of 2014. I decided to fly to Arizona for the training and combined this with a visit to some extended family I had not seen in years.

This approach was demonstrated by Larry and Alfred numerous times with volunteers from our training group. To witness the change in these volunteer participants using the BSFF treatment modality was powerful and helped move me from some initial skepticism to a believer in potential for healing in this approach.

One of the benefits of BSFF is its portability. Clients are free to use this procedure on their own outside of sessions.

One key to the BSFF approach lies in the power of intention. This is another dimension of the self that was impacted by the Fall and/or in some of our own brokenness through various wounding experiences. It is wonderful to see the power of intention be redeemed and restored in such a positive healing manner.

42
CHAPTER

INVISIBLE REALITIES

Truth reveals reality, and reality can be described as what we humans run into when we are wrong, a collision in which we always lose.

Dallas Willard

Who or what are we going to give permission to be able to influence, mold, and shape us? What is the story you are living in? If truth is that which corresponds to reality, are you confident that the beliefs that you are betting your life on are rock-solid?

Being mistaken about life, the things of God, and the human soul is a deadly serious matter.

Dallas Willard

I attended a conference in the 70's where one of the keynote speakers was Dr. Anthony Campolo, sociologist and activist. We forget much of what we hear and read over the years, but there are statements that seem to hit us with a force that makes them hard to forget.

Here is one of his statements that day at the conference that had an indelible impact on me:

> *We will either be led by the Spirit (of God) or manipulated by the culture.*

Really?

In his book, *Hearing God,* Dallas Willard writes:

> The greatest divide between human beings and human cultures is between those who regard the physical world as being of primary importance and those who do not, between those who view what is visible as all that's real or at least the touchstone of reality, and those who do not. Today, we live in a culture that overwhelmingly gives primary, if not exclusive importance to the visible. This stance is incorporated in the power structures that permeate our world and is disseminated by the education system and government.
>
> But neither God, nor the human mind and heart are visible. It is so with *all truly personal reality.* "No one has ever seen the Father," Jesus reminds us. And while you know more about your own mind and heart than you could ever say, little to none of it was learned through sensory perception. God and **the self** accordingly meet in the *invisible* world because they *are* invisible *by nature* [emphasis added].[127]

What do you believe is true and ultimately real? Another way of saying this is,

"What is the story that I am actually believing?" [128]

Many people tend to avoid challenging questions like these, preferring rather to live out a false self in an illusory world of their own creation. I would like to challenge you to give some serious attention and attempt to honestly answer the following questions:

Who is the Bad Guy?

How do you explain evil in the world?

Who is the Hero?

Who or what are you looking to, to save the day?

Where does hope lie?

Are you confident your future is absolutely wonderful? [129]

For the repentant, committed Christ follower who believes in what has been revealed in the Bible, the ultimate answer to all these questions is quite clear.

With a humble dependence on the Christian God that keeps his promises, I am confident that my future is absolutely wonderful. I may not be able to experience and achieve all that I would like to in this life. While that may produce some sorrow and sadness in the here and now . . . there is an incredible life to come for the Christ follower to look forward to that truly is absolutely wonderful.

> *He will wipe every tear from their eyes. There will be no more death or mourning or crying or pain, for the old order of things has passed away.*
>
> Revelation 21:4 (NIV)

> *No eye has seen, nor hear has heard, no mind has conceived what God has prepared for those who love him.*
>
> I Corinthians 2:9 (NIV)

43
CHAPTER

THE EMMAUS EXAMPLE

This account is found in Luke 24:13–35ff. To summarize, two individuals were on a journey. They were walking and conversing with one another. Jesus, resurrected from the dead, approached and began traveling with them, but they did not recognize Him.

Jesus asked them questions, inviting them into a dialogue. He seemed to express frustration at them for failing to recognize all that had happened. "And beginning with Moses and with all the prophets, He explained to them the things concerning himself in all the Scriptures" (v. 27).

They were about to arrive at the village. The day was almost over. They invited Him to stay with them, and He joined them. During the evening meal, He took the bread, blessed it, broke it, and began giving it to them.

"Their eyes were opened, they recognized Him, then he vanished from their sight."

Experiential: "were not our hearts burning within us when He was speaking to us."

It is my hope for all who read this that you may have an Emmaus-like experience at some point in your life.

44

IN SUMMARY, AND TO SIMPLIFY

Wisdom (mental dimension)

"Do you want be healed?" We must answer this question well, first.

Dan Allender said, "The only precondition for change is a desire for something more."

If we are content to live in our broken, unhealed state, nothing will change. As long as we remain blind to our true condition, nothing will change. In order to receive healing and to be able to care accurately and skillfully, you have to be aware of what needs healing and restoration.

Dallas Willard said, "Care requires understanding."

"What do you want me to do for you?" (Matthew 20:32b).

Stature (Physical Dimension)

For some, if you are walking around with substantial imbalances in your brain and body, these need to be addressed first. For example, if you have a thyroid imbalance, this will need to be addressed skillfully and, well, first. (Remember my own story?)

To what extent is physical/physiological healing available to you in this lifetime? What will God's sovereignly permit or allow for you to be more conformed into His image?

Favor with God (Spiritual Dimension)

This is potential capacity to enter more fully into a relationship with God. There are some incredibly rich resources available today in this area.

Favor with Man (Social Dimension)

All of this occurs in a context of attachment love and a healing dialogue with God and at least one person of understanding. "The purposes of a man's heart are deep waters, but a man of understanding draws them out" (Proverbs 20:5 NIV). Authentic community is vital.

45

THE GREAT COMMANDMENT
AND THE GREAT COMMISSION

It is what I believe to be a biblically sound belief and contention that an important part of Jesus' mission on earth was to "bind up the brokenhearted." I also have contended that this is a very important ministry of healing and restoration for us all and it is impossible to go through this life without getting broken.

I have presented the argument that this ministry of healing is a priority, especially if you believe the order of divine revelation matters. If by the grace of God we seek to become a more substantially healed, whole person through healing the various aspects of our broken selves, then, by logical extension, we may very well have greater capacity for the Great Commandment.[130] "Love the Lord your God with all your heart and with all your soul and with all your mind'. This is the first and greatest commandment. And the second is like it, 'Love your neighbor as yourself.'"

Finally, it is my contention that a more substantially healed, whole true self is quite possibly in a more prepared condition to fulfill the Great Commission.[131]

"Therefore go and make disciples of all the nations, baptizing them in the name of the Father and of the Son and of the Holy Spirit, and teaching them to obey everything I have commanded you. And surely I am with you always, to the very end of the age."

The Lord bless you, and keep you;
The Lord make His face shine on you,
And be gracious to you;
The Lord lift up His countenance on you;
And give you peace.

Numbers 6:24-26 (NASB)

ACKNOWLEDGMENTS

Where do I start?

Thanks be to God for His many and varied gracious gifts, far too many for me to count.

Thanks to my parents, whom this book is dedicated to, along with the rest of my family of origin: brother, Larry Arnold (now deceased); sister, Dr. Joy Arnold-Morse, dentist; and brother, Jim Arnold, full-time Christian missionary to Thailand. My life has been immeasurably enriched by them and their respective families. Thanks to the rich extended family I have experienced life with on both the Arnold and Smith sides.

Irene Nagaraj reviewed what I had written in the early stages of this process. Her comments and suggestions were invaluable. Sam Quick reviewed my manuscript when it was closer to completion. His affirmation about the importance of the topic and overall encouragement for what I had written was received like fresh wind in my sails. Andy Rector provided some helpful editorial assistance, and my thanks to Daniel Gilliam, Timothy Gilliam, and Marc Gritton for invaluable technical support in this project.

Special thanks in this Revised Edition goes to Allen Arnold for his assistance with better flow and organization, Chris Diggs for the creative cover design, and finally, to Keri Barnum with New Shelves Books for all her assistance in making this a great publishing experience.

Thanks to every church family I have had the privilege to be a part of. They have provided both a community and a container as I have healed—and continue to heal—from aspects of my own brokenness.

Thanks to the church universal, other various Christian ministries, plus other organizations and institutions that have touched my life in meaningful ways: Wild At Heart, Our Daily Bread, Ministries of Pastoral Care, The Allender Center, and the Amen Clinics, to name a few.

Thanks to my friends over the years in different places. Mentioning all of you would be more than a challenge, so unfortunately many names will be left out. I may mention a few names in telling parts of my story.

Thanks to the clinical and administrative staff at North Springs Counseling. Working with such a great group is a joy and a privilege. We know we are engaged in serious business, but the camaraderie we have is enriching, encouraging, and also quite a bit of fun!

Thanks to the family I come home to at night. Susan, I love you, and thanks for putting up with me!

RESOURCES

Chapter 7
Elaine N. Aron, *The Highly Sensitive Person*, www.hsperson.com

Chapter 8
Richard Winter, *Perfecting Ourselves to Death*
David Seamands, *Healing Grace*
Brene' Brown, *The Gifts of Imperfection*

Chapter 19
Thomas Merton, *New Seeds of Contemplation*
David G. Benner, *The Gift of Being Yourself*
Brennan Manning with Jim Hancock, *Posers, Fakers, and Wannabes (Unmasking the Real You)*

Chapter 27
Healing for Damaged Emotions and *Healing of Memories* by David A. Seamands
The Healing Presence and *Restoring the Christian Soul* by Leanne Payne
www.wildatheart.org or the Wild at Heart app, "Prayers We Pray"
Siang Yang Tan, "Inner Healing"[132]

Chapter 29
Janet Chester Bly, *Awakening Your Sense of Wonder*.
Richard Beck, *Hunting Magic Eels*

Chapter 32
Amen Clinics, www.amenclinics.com
Brain MD, www.brainMD.com
Brain Health Assessment, www.brainhealthassessment.com

Chapter 33
ADD Type Test, www.addtypetest.com

END NOTES

1. Isaiah 61:1 (NIV).

2. Luke 4:18–21 (NIV).

3. In the Lukan quotation of this passage, the words "to bind up the brokenhearted" are omitted from several important ancient Greek manuscripts of Luke. Other ancient Greek texts include these words. In the latter manuscripts, the phrase has probably been reinserted by later editors on the basis of the Isaiah text in the Greek LXX (Septuagint), the standard Old Testament text in use by the early Christians. The sentiment, "bind up the brokenhearted," however, is certainly implied by the Lukan quotation (Dr. Jerry Gladson, Richmont Graduate University).

4. Ibid.

5. John 5:39–40 (NASB).

6. Edward Mote, "The Solid Rock," 1834.

7. Hebrew; Septuagint, *the blind*.

8. Mark W. Baker, *Jesus, the Greatest Therapist Who Ever Lived* (New York: HarperCollins Publishers, 2007), 67.

9. *It's a Wonderful Life* (1946).

10. A possible exception to this is being in a physically or emotionally destructive relationship where some may have to take slower steps over time to ensure their own safety.

11. "By Permission. From Merriam-Webster.com ©2019 by Merriam-Webster, Inc. https://www.merriam-webster.com/dictionary/ "

12. *Life Coaching* DVD course through AACC.

13. Mark W. Baker, *Jesus: The Greatest Therapist Who Ever Lived* (New York: Harper Collins, 2007), 67.

14. Bright, Bill, *The Four Spiritual Laws*, p.2 (1965). Campus Crusade for Christ, Inc.

15. Wilder, Jim. *Renovated: God, Dallas Willard, and the Church that Transforms*. p.6 (2020) Shepherd's House/NavPress.

16. The L'abri Statements, p. 4.

17. Hebrew Words, NASB95, *brokenhearted*, exported from Logos Bible Software.

18. Bible Word Study, *heart*, Hebrew Words, NASB95, exported from Logos Bible Software.

19. Exported from Logos Bible Software, בֵל lēḇ, the heart.

20. Translation, NASB95. Exported from Logos Bible Software.

21. F. Brown, S. R. Driver, and C. A. Briggs, *Enhanced Brown-Driver-Briggs Hebrew and English Lexicon* (Oxford: Clarendon Press, 1977).

22. W. L. Holladay and L. Köhler, *A Concise Hebrew and Aramaic Lexicon of the Old Testament* (Leiden: Brill, 2000). Exported from Logos Bible Software, 12:50 p.m. August 12, 2017.

23. David A. Seamands, *The Healing of Memories* (SP Publications, 1985), 98–99.

24. John 14:6; PeaceWithGod.net; *Invitation to a Journey* by M. Robert Mulholland Jr. (Expanded by Ruth Haley Barton)

25. Mark 8:29 (NIV).

26. Acts 9:4 (NASB).

27. Joachim Neander, "Praise Ye the Lord, the Almighty."

28. "The Myers and Briggs Foundation," www.myersbriggs.org.

29. Susan Cain, *Quiet* (New York: Random House, Inc., 2012, 2013), 3.

30. Adam S. McHugh, *Introverts in the Church* (InterVarsity Press, 2009), 34–35.

31. Ibid., 35–36.

32. Adam S. McHugh, 37–38.

33. Ibid., 41.

34. Ibid.

35. Bellarmine University (2015), billboard advertisement.

36. Adam S. McHugh, 42.

37. Ibid., 50.

38. Ibid., 55–56.

39. Ibid., 57–58.

40. Stella Chess and Alexander Thomas, *Temperament in Clinical Practice* (The Guilford Press, 1986), 4.

41. "The Highly Sensitive Person," www.hsperson.com.

42. Elaine N. Aron, *The Highly Sensitive Person* (Harmony Books, 1996,1998), 27.

43. Preface, *The Highly Sensitive Person*, xiv.

44. Ibid., 10–11.

45. Richard Winter, *Perfecting Ourselves to Death* (InterVarsity Press, 2005), 88.

46. Ibid., 33.

47. Gerald W. Johnson, *Called to Command* (Paducah: Turner Publishing Company, 1996), 15–16.

48. *Perfecting Ourselves to Death*, 33.

49. "Understanding Behavioral Individuality," https://www.b-di.com/ctsindex.html.

50. www.brainMD.com.

51. Daniel Amen, *Change Your Brain, Change Your Life* (New York: Harmony Books, 1998, 2015). www.amenclinics.com.

52. Ephesians 2:8–10 (NIV).

53. *Seizures after Traumatic Brain Injury* (2010), Model Systems Knowledge Translation Center.

54. David G. Benner, *The Gift of Being Yourself* (Downers Grove, Ill.: 2004, 2015), 24.

55. Webster's Third New International Dictionary, Unabridged, "Mind."

56. Timothy Keller, *The Reason for God* (New York: Penguin Group, 2008), Introduction, xvii.

57. Matthew 11:11 (NIV).

58. Matthew 14:3–5 (NIV).

59. Matthew 11:3 (NLT).

60. Josh McDowell, *More Than a Carpenter* (Josh McDowell Ministry, 1977, 2005, 2009), 70–88.

61. Ibid., 87.

62. Jeremiah 29:13 (NIV).

63. Hebrews 12:1 (NASB).

64. Dallas Willard, *The Divine Conspiracy* (New York: HarperCollins Publishers, 1997), 138–139.

65. E. M. Bartlett, "Victory In Jesus," 1939.

66. Webster's Third New International Dictionary, Unabridged, "Spirit."

67. Dallas Willard, *Renovation of the Heart* (Colorado Springs: NavPress, 2002, 2012), 29.

68. John Nolland, "Preface," in *The Gospel of Matthew: A Commentary on the Greek Text* (Grand Rapids: Carlisle, W. B. Eerdmans, Paternoster Press, 2005), 912.

69. W. E. Vine, MA, was a classical scholar, skilled expositor, and trustworthy theologian. He was recognized internationally for his outstanding Greek scholarship. His *Expository Dictionary of New Testament Words*, first published in 1939, represents the fruit of his lifetime labors and is an unsurpassed classic in its field.

70. Dallas Willard, *The Spirit of the Disciplines: Understanding How God Changes Lives* (New York: HarperCollins Publishers, 1988), 54.

71. Daniel Amen, M.D.

72. *The Four Streams* CD set available through Wild at Heart (www.wildatheart.org).

73. M. Scott Peck, *The Road Less Travelled*.

74. John Ortberg, *Soul Keeping: Caring for The Most Important Part of You* (Grand Rapids: Zondervan, 2014), 23.

75. Webster's Third New International Dictionary, Unabridged, "Distort."

76. Ibid., 30.

77. Ibid.

78. Ibid.

79. Ibid., 31.

80. Ibid., 31–32.

81. Ibid., 34.

82. Ibid., 34–35.

83. Psalm 103:5 (NIV).

84. John 4:10–14 (NIV).

85. David G. Benner, 83.

86. Ibid.

87. Ibid., 84.

88. K. H. Rengstorf, ἑταῖρος. G. Kittel, G. W. Bromiley, and G. Friedrich (eds.), *Theological Dictionary of the New Testament*, volume 2. (Grand Rapids: Eerdmans), 698–699.

89. M. J. Harris, *The Second Epistle to the Corinthians: A Commentary on the Greek Text* (Grand Rapids: Milton Keynes, UK, W. B. Eerdmans Pub. Co., Paternoster Press, 2005), 358–360.

90. Caroline Leaf, 79–80.

91. *Internet Evangelism Update*, PeaceWithGod.net, Billy Graham Evangelistic Association (January 2017).

92. David A. Seamands, *Healing for Damaged Emotions* (Wheaton, Ill.: SP Publications, Inc., 1981), 13.

93. Luke 22:31–32 (NIV).

94. John 21:1–23 (NIV).

95. Romans 1:21 (NASB).

96. Swanson, J. (1997). *Dictionary of Biblical Languages with Semantic Domains: Hebrew (Old Testament)* (electronic ed.). Oak Harbor: Logos Research Systems, Inc. Exported from Logos Bible Software, 5:01 p.m. December 28, 2015.

97. Dallas Willard, *Hearing God* (Downers Grove, Ill.: InterVarsity Press, 1999, 2012), 155–188.

98. Caroline Leaf, *Switch on Your Brain* (Grand Rapids: Baker Books, 2013), 15.

99. Earl Henslin, *This Is Your Brain in Love* (Nashville: Thomas Nelson, 2009), 31.

100. Luke 10:27 (NASB).

101. Ibid.

102. John Eldredge, *Prayer for Inner Healing*, www.wildatheart.org.

103. "Spiritual Direction: The Holy Spirit and Christian Spirituality in Counseling and Psychotherapy" (Tan, 2011), AACC Live Webinar April 17, 2012.

104. Archibald D. Hart, *Sleep, It Does a Family Good* (Carol Stream: Tyndale House Publishers, 2010), 9–10.

105. Ibid., 10–11.

106. Leanne Payne, *Restoring the Christian Soul* (Grand Rapids: Baker Books, 1991), 25.

107. Matthew 16:21 (NASB).

108. Matthew 16:24–26 (NEB).

109. Leanne Payne, *Restoring the Christian Soul*, 26.

110. Ibid., 51.

111. Ibid, 23–24.

112. David A. Seamands, *Healing for Damaged Emotions* (Wheaton, Ill.: SP Publications, 1981), 33.

113. John Ortberg, *Soul Keeping* (Zondervan, 2014), 62.

114. A *nutraceutical* is a nutrient with medicinal properties. Harvard researchers call them "standardized, pharmaceutical grade nutrients." Live presentation by Parris M. Kidd, PhD, chief science officer and director of quality, Brain MD Health titled, "Why (and How) Everyone Should Take Nutraceutical Supplements to Help Optimize Their Brain and Body," Amen Clinic presentation in Nashville, July 22, 2017.

115. Webster's Third New International Dictionary, Unabridged, "Attention."

116. Tyrosine from brainMD by Daniel Amen, MD, www. brainmd.com.

117. John Eldredge, *Waking the Dead* (Nashville: Thomas Nelson Publishers, 2003).

118. John 21:25 (NIV)

119. 2 Corinthians 12:8–9 (NIV).

120. Reference?

121. Jamie Marich, *EMDR Made Simple* (Eau Claire: Premier Publishing & Media, 2011), 19.

122. Ibid. 41.

123. Ibid., 48–49.

124. Ibid., 45.

125. Larry P. Nims, *BSFF Treatment Protocol* (Goodyear: 2007–2014), 2. This handout was a part of the BSFF training in Phoenix, Arizona, in 2014.

126. Caroline Leaf, *Switch On Your Brain* (Grand Rapids: Baker Books, 2013), 79–80.

127. Dallas Willard, *Hearing God* (Downers Grove, IL: InterVarsity Press, 2012), 284-285.

128. John Eldredge, *"30 Days to Resilience"* (PauseApp.com).

129. Ibid.

130. Matthew 22:37–39 (NIV).

131. Matthew 28:19–20 (NIV).

132. "Spiritual Direction: The Holy Spirit and Christian Spirituality in Counseling and Psychotherapy" (Tan, 2011), AACC Live Webinar April 17, 2012.